THE GOVERNMENT
OF THE
GERMAN FEDERAL
REPUBLIC

Harper's Comparative Government Series

MICHAEL CURTIS, EDITOR

THE GOVERNMENT
OF THE
GERMAN FEDERAL
REPUBLIC

ROBERT G. NEUMANN

PROFESSOR OF POLITICAL SCIENCE
UNIVERSITY OF CALIFORNIA, LOS ANGELES

HARPER & ROW
Publishers
NEW YORK, EVANSTON, AND LONDON

Library of Congress Catalog Card Number: 66-22517

To the Memory of My Father

CONTENTS

PREFACE ix

ONE / The German Nation and the German Reich 1

TWO / Destruction and Rebirth 19

THREE / Once More a State 31

FOUR / Political Life 37

FIVE / The Constitutional Fabric of the German Federal Republic 87

SIX / Civil Liberties 95

SEVEN / Executive Power 102

EIGHT / The Legislature 118

NINE / The Judiciary 143

TEN / *Land* and Local Government 154

ELEVEN / A Concluding Look at Germany 163

A SELECTED BIBLIOGRAPHY 168

INDEX 181

PREFACE

NIETZSCHE SAID that there is something peculiar about the Germans inasmuch as whatever one says about them, one is bound to be at least partially right. This remark, which need not be taken at face value, nevertheless underlines the fact that there have been violent upheavals and drastic reversals in German history which have caused the German people, at one time or another, to look in many different directions.

Perhaps no other generation of any other country has tried as hard as does the present young German generation to overcome its past; yet the past will be with them for quite some time to come, if for no other reason than that no other nation is faced by the same necessities. Italy has Fascism to live down, but although Fascism lasted much longer than Nazism, it did not indulge in mass extermination despite much individual cruelty, nor was it claimed to be the product of a long historical development as was Nazism.

Germany's past has to be understood in order for one to understand its present; but no claim is made here that the present is simply the product of the past. On the contrary, much of the present has been forged deliberately in order to avoid the courses of the past. But for that, too, the past must be understood. Hence, a somewhat larger proportion of this book is devoted to history than might otherwise be warranted.

Germany's evolution differs in many significant respects from that of other European countries. It had forged a mighty supranational empire, the Holy Roman Empire, before others built empires, yet that thousand-year-long development served to retard rather than to promote German unification. When unification came, it arrived as an event long dreamed of and long wished for, and was quickly accepted as natural and immutable. Alas, it lasted only 74 years, from 1871 to 1945, before the country became once more divided. Yet unification, however shortlived, has so thoroughly entered German consciousness that its disappearance is deeply felt as a profound hurt, an unnatural deed, which looms ever larger in Germany's political thoughts and acts. No early end of this division is in sight, though it corresponds in no way to German wishes, East or West, and hence there is a permanent element of dissatisfaction in Germany's domestic and foreign policy which raises many difficult and delicate problems.

Yet Germany is the most populous, the most industrially powerful country of Europe, especially of Western Europe, and its twelve divisions of troops constitute the only sizable, conventional, contribution to the Western defense and to NATO outside the massive American strength. The German Federal Republic is also the third largest economic power in the world. Hence the delicate and difficult problems stemming from Germany's division are inescapably problems of deep concern to the entire West and in fact to the world.

This slender volume attempts to explain the political life and the institutions of West Germany, of the German Federal Republic only. Communist East Germany, the so-called "German Democratic Republic" (DDR) is neither "German" nor "democratic" but a Soviet satellite whose institutions have been imported from the outside. Although conditions there have undoubtedly improved in recent years, it is, and remains, more alien and more subjugate than the other Communist countries of Eastern Europe, being more dependent than are they on support by the Soviet Union. An analysis of the DDR would, therefore, fit more properly into a book dealing with the governments of Communist Eastern Europe.

This book is presented to the public after Chancellor Konrad Adenauer has left the position of head of the German federal government although, as these lines are written, he remains a powerful political factor in his country and his party. His imperious personality, his extraordinary political talent, dominated the first 14 years of the German Federal Republic to such an extent that it became difficult to say which were the institutions and what was just Adenauer in the new state. Now that he has been replaced by quite a different type of personality, the permanent institutions and political habits of the Federal Republic are emerging with greater clarity.

The author has had the good fortune of meeting and knowing most of modern Germany's political leaders; to them and to their less well known but often no less well informed colleagues, as well as to many German academicians, journalists, and other thoughtful individuals, he owes a profound debt of gratitude. They have all contributed to his understanding of their country However, for all conclusions and errors the author bears sole responsibility. All the works consulted are cited in the bibliography at the end of the book.

Finally the author wishes to express his appreciation to his diligent research assistant, Mrs. Anne Bodenheimer, and to his former secretary, Mrs. Trudy Woods, for taking many onerous burdens off his hands. Thanks are also due to Mrs. Christa Eichhorn who typed the first draft of the manuscript. But the author's deepest gratitude goes to his wife for invaluable editorial, critical, and other assistance.

ROBERT G. NEUMANN

THE GOVERNMENT
OF THE
GERMAN FEDERAL
REPUBLIC

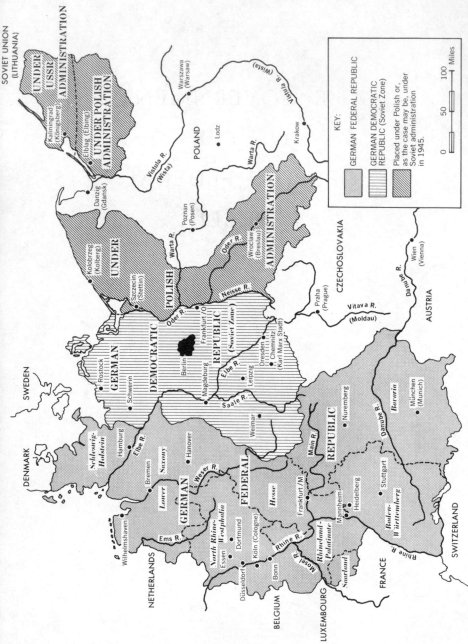

CHAPTER ONE

The German Nation
and the German Reich

THERE IS one theme which persistently recurs in German history, that of national unity. It is the dominant theme still. A nation is neither a state nor a civilization, nor is it necessarily identical with a linguistic or cultural group. Rather it is an agglomeration of people who, through historical experiences and growth, as well as by the evolution of common ideas, have become *politically* conscious that they belong together. Ernest Renan expressed this romantically when he said: "A nation represents a spiritual principle, resulting from the profound complications of history, a spiritual family, not a group determined by the shape of the land." Benjamin Disraeli defined the nation more briefly but no less sensitively as "a work of art and time." As Conze stated, the German nation, therefore, is not composed of all those whose native tongue is German and who adhere to German culture, but only of those who consciously experience membership therein.

A nation so conceived is not an absolutely fixed entity; it is, as Renan stated so aptly, " a constantly repeated plebiscite." A nation may be divided, even split up into many parts, and yet remain a nation. But, on the other hand, an attempt to unify a nation on a "folkish," "racial," or linguistic basis, such as Hitler tried with Germany, may end in unmitigated disaster.

I have said that nation and language need not coincide. Nevertheless, language is important as a powerful, unifying element. It was in the 10th Century that a largely linguistic sense of being German began to be felt in the area we know as Germany, and a literature in the vernacular appeared, especially the popular "Theodisk" which, in its latinized version, became known as

1

"Lingua Teutonica." Still, one could not speak of a common language when the Saxon tongue was much more like the one spoken by the Anglo-Saxons on the British Isles than like that of the neighboring inhabitants of Franconia. Only in the 15th Century did the term "German Nation" become current. By that time the curious structure which history was later to call "the Holy Roman Empire of the German Nation" had existed several hundreds of years, but the basic concept of that empire did not coincide with the unifying influence of the language.

Already in the 6th Century A.D. the Frankish tribe or "nation" (gens) had created an empire through the submission and acquisition of many other regions and peoples. After a period of decay, the Frankish Empire rose again and acquired quite unprecedented glory and power when on Christmas Eve, 800, Charlemagne had the imperial crown placed on his head. It was a fateful crown for it was neither "German" nor "Frankish," but "Roman," and the coronation took place in Rome. It was a deliberate attempt to recreate the myth of the Roman Empire whose 700 years of history had remained in the memory of man as an enviable period of peace and well-being. By making this coronation both Roman and Christian, notice was served to the world that this Empire was not a tribal nor regional affair but that it had universal aspirations throughout Christendom.

Few historical events have been more fateful, more long-lasting, or on the whole more unfortunate in their consequences. This empire was neither holy, nor Roman, nor even of the German nation. Although most Germans lived within it, a good many lived outside, while many other nations and nationalities lived within its borders, from Danes to Italians, and from Frenchmen to Poles. One whole non-German nation, the Czechs, lived entirely within the frontiers of the "Reich."[1]

The fiction of the "Roman" Empire required the correlation,

---

[1] The word Reich defies accurate translation. It is derived from the Latin word *regnum* and is exactly equivalent neither to "empire," "commonwealth," nor "state." It has historically constituted a German dream of a realm which lies both in reality and in ideas. It could be called a historical myth more than a constitutional or territorial entity. The father of the Weimar Constitution of 1919, Hugo Preuss, insisted on the retention of the word Reich because of the traditional and emotional values attached to it in the minds of the German people.

and in many instances the virtual reconquest of Italy with the election of every new emperor.[2] This required considerable effort on the part of the princes of the realm, who had to raise the required soldiers. They used this effort to consolidate their own feudal powers to such an extent that by the 13th Century they had become legally and, in fact, undisputed masters in their respective principalities. The constant conflict of the emperors with the Popes gave the princes additional opportunity to take sides and, thereby, increase and consolidate their privileges. At the same time in England, royal judges were eliminating feudal jurisdiction, and in France, the Capetian monarchs were accumulating unprecedented power and centralized authority for the crown. Germany was going in the opposite direction: her monarchs neglected consolidation at home, while pursuing a dream in Italy. When the strangely romantic and poetry-writing (in Italian) Frederick II died in Palermo in 1250, it was not only the virtual end of the Hohenstauffen dynasty but also the end of the pretense of a universal empire.[3]

Even as a German empire, rather than a universal one, this realm was not thereafter held with much success, despite moments of greatness. The Thirty Years War was a civil as well as international war and tore the country to pieces, decimating its inhabitants to a degree unsurpassed by any later war.[4] The Westphalian Peace (Münster and Osnabrück, 1648) conferred "sovereignty" on the feudal lords, several of whom were foreign

[2] The German emperors were elected by an assembly of certain ecclesiastic and temporal princes who were called "electors" (Kurfürsten). For most of the life of the Holy Roman Empire they were the Archbishops of Mainz, Trier, and Cologne, the King of Bohemia, the Margrave of Brandenburg, the Duke of Saxony, and the Palatine of the Rhine.

[3] As a ruling dynasty, the Hohenstaufens ended 1254 with Konrad IV (whose rule was disputed). The last Hohenstaufen, Konradin, was executed in Naples in 1268.

[4] The Thirty Years War (1618 to 1648) was probably the most cruel and destructive of all times. Being essentially a civil war, it was not fought along fixed frontiers or clear front lines but raged all over Germany. As the war dragged on, the commanders on both sides fell back more and more upon the looting of towns and villages to obtain their supplies and pay their professional soldiers. While battle losses were considerable and such massacres as that of Magdeburg were common, the greatest losses probably came from privation and disease. When the war was over all Germany was devastated and did not recover in its enterprise, as well as in culture and art, for a full century.

potentates. The imperial crown survived, but only to lead a shadowy existence without reality. It came to an official end in 1806 when the Napoleonic wars shattered what was left of German unity.[5]

Meanwhile the period between 1648 and 1806 marked the final decline of Austria as a power in Germany. Her place was taken eventually, but not immediately, by Prussia. Historic folklore has long regarded Prussia as the embodiment of all that is undesirable in the German character, but the facts are more complex. Prussia was a relative newcomer to German history. Long after the establishment of the Holy Roman Empire, the central and eastern provinces of the Reich were inhabited by lawless pagan tribes of predominantly Slavic origin called *Pruzzen* who preyed upon their more civilized, and hence wealthier, neighbors, the Poles. All attempts to control them having failed, a Polish duke, Conrad of Masovia, appealed for help to the Order of Teutonic Knights, a religious as well as military organization, which in a long series of battles (1226–1283) defeated the aborigines and absorbed their territory. Christianization and Germanic settlements proved particularly effective in East Prussia.

The Teutonic Knights in turn became an irritant to their neighbors and were defeated at the Battle of Tannenberg (1410), being saved from total annihilation only by the diplomatic skill of their chief (*Hochmeister*) Henry of Plauen. After a new revolt of the Prussian (Slavic) nobles who obtained help from Poland, the Teutonic Order was forced to cede West Prussia and Ermeland to Poland, but retained East Prussia as a Polish fief. Thus was created the "corridor" problem which later plagued German-Polish relations for many years.

In 1525 the last *Hochmeister* renounced his Catholic faith, became a Protestant, and was created the first Duke of Prussia by his uncle, the Duke of Poland. This Duchy of Prussia and the Margravate of Brandenburg were united in 1618 to form the nucleus of the later Prussian power. Other territories were gained in the Westphalian Peace of 1648, and in 1660 Frederick Wil-

[5] In 1804 Francis II (Habsburg) proclaimed himself hereditary Emperor of Austria (under the name of Francis I) and in 1806 he renounced the title and crown of Germany. With this act, the "Holy Roman Empire of the German Nation" came officially to an end.

liam, the "Great Elector," forced Poland to renounce its nominal overlordship over Prussia. He also obtained other territory, especially far to the west in the Ruhr. His son, Frederick I, was the first king of Prussia (1701–1713).

The Prussian kings had learned from the mistakes of the emperors. The local nobility (*Junkers*) lost all vestiges of independence, but in return received superior positions in the newly formed professional army.[6] Frederick William I (1713–1740) and his son, Frederick II, "the Great" (1740–1786), forged an army of exceptional efficiency with which Frederick II embarked on a long power struggle in which all inconvenient treaties, agreements, or promises were cast aside. Despite many notable feats of arms and generalship, Prussian diplomacy proved unequal to the task of evading the consequences of rapidly shifting alliances. Erstwhile friends and foes began to form a united front against Prussia, and would surely have crushed Frederick had he not been saved by the timely death of an enemy, the Empress Elizabeth of Russia, and the coming to power of an admirer, Peter III.

Frederick II, like his father, was an absolute ruler; a later period might have called him a king-dictator. His ministers and generals were his secretaries and lieutenants. But his absolutism was not generally arbitrary. The laws, once adopted, applied to all in equal manner. The civil service and the army were efficient and incorruptible.

To modern generations, absolutism may seem too high a price to pay for efficiency, orderliness, and the equal application of laws. But to the 18th Century, there were solid advantages. The people took to the idea of "Law and Order" which gave the subject few rights, but allowed him to sleep peacefully in his bed if he had obeyed all laws and commands—not an inconsiderable blessing in those days. Thus Prussia was able to create what the emperors had failed to create, namely a sense of unity and of pride. This unity appeared in the form of a pyramid headed by a solidly installed authority which took care of all matters and

---

[6] The name *Junker* is derived from the Middle High German *junc-Herre* (the young master). The title was originally attributed to the sons of princes and rulers but later the name *Junker* (pronounced "yoonker") became a general term covering the Prussian nobility, especially of the agrarian and military kind.

supplied all the answers. Despite violence and upheaval elsewhere, Prussia remained untroubled, but, while it prevented its citizens from committing the bloodshed and horror of the French Revolution, it also prevented them from absorbing any "radical" ideas about popular sovereignty, self-government, and the rights of man.

Later, when Napoleon's armies occupied large parts of Germany, the ideas of the French Revolution did enter, but they were confined largely to intellectuals and dissident members of the middle and upper classes. The large masses of the people were hardly affected. Some heroic struggles, and especially the unsuccessful Revolution of 1848, were therefore stillborn and left few traces. Today, in retrospect, the gathering at St. Paul's Church in Frankfurt in 1848 (the German National Assembly) is often celebrated as the birth of German liberalism. In all fairness one must agree that the upright and often tragically heroic men who gathered there also represented an aspect of Prussia. But what prevailed for many years thereafter was the supervening idea of authority and efficiency, rather than of liberty.

Still it is well not to measure too quickly with modern tools. Authority, as the Prussians knew it, was not liberal in any sense of the word. But compared to the total arbitrariness of modern dictatorships, whether Nazi, Fascist, or Communist, the "orderly" and "lawful" authoritarianism of the Prussian tradition did not assault human dignity and did not prevent the rise of controversial ideas, including those of Marx and Engels.

German nationalism, which rose strongly from the emotions of the Napoleonic wars, was originally liberal. By extolling the nation, it proclaimed the equality of its citizens, a concept which was not in agreement with the feudal ideas of the ruling princes and lords. The powers of those days—above all the Prussian king and the all-powerful Austrian minister, Prince Metternich—saw in German nationalism a danger to the "legitimate" thrones. When the French Revolution of 1848 occurred, the spark quickly jumped over to Germany in a quite spontaneous manner. But the Revolution, so to speak, came to a halt in front of the throne and thus failed because, in the final showdown, the masses of the German people and especially of Germany's middle class society, preferred order and authority to liberty, which was suspected of being tied to disorder. Later, in 1871, at the end of the Franco-

Prussian war, the ideal of German nationalism, German unity, was indeed achieved at long last. But it was not fought over and conquered by revolutionaries and reformers; it was the accomplishment of the military and civil service groups, especially of the remarkable Chancellor, Prince Otto von Bismarck. Thus the principle of authority had again been affirmed and those who upheld it felt richly rewarded.

The period after German unification in 1871 coincided with Germany's rapid industrialization and fast rise in economic development as a world power. These achievements were inevitably tied to the prevailing system of government and social order, and those who assailed this order were thus easily identified with forces who would undermine or at least endanger all these achievements. Nationalism had now become separated from liberalism and was turning in quite a different direction.

The operetta-like figure of Emperor William II, with his bombastic and frequently silly pronouncements, has distorted the public image of the "second Empire" but this does it less than justice.[7] While Bismarck, the "Iron Chancellor," was at the helm it represented quite a remarkable construction. It was a federation in which the various principalities or *Laender* retained considerable rights. It was dominated not so much by the Emperor as by Prussia, which comprised two-thirds of the territory of the Empire. And Prussia, whose king was also German Emperor, whose Prime Minister was also German Chancellor, and whose bureaucracy had largely become the bureaucracy of the Empire, was archconservative, essentially Protestant, and authoritarian in tendency. Prussian authoritarianism was mild, however, by the standards of modern dictatorship. The freedom of speech, press, and assembly were frequently interfered with but never entirely suppressed. And even during the height of the anti-socialist and anti-Catholic legislation and repressive measures, the two parties concerned, the Social Democratic Party and the Center Party, were never outlawed, continued to present and elect members to Parliament and, in fact, emerged much strengthened by the

[7] The "Holy Roman Empire" is regarded as the first "Reich;" the Empire which emerged from the Franco-Prussian War in 1871 and was essentially Bismarck's work is regarded as the second Reich; and Hitler proclaimed his rule as the "Third Reich."

struggle when it came to an end. In foreign affairs, although popularly identified with the "blood and iron" image, Bismarck was a prudent leader who struck hard but made mild peace treaties, and never failed to do his utmost to convert vanquished foes into allies if at all possible.

The carefully balanced foreign policy of Bismarck came to an end when the incompetent William II "dropped the pilot" in 1890. Bismarck's ability to combine strength with moderation, and in particular with a sense of limitation for Germany, was not conspicuous among the talents of his successors. In domestic affairs too, there remained a fateful gap. The Second Empire gave its citizens considerable, though not complete, political freedom and installed universal manhood suffrage at an early time. But the government remained responsible to the Emperor rather than the voters or the voters' representatives, the members of Parliament. As a result, much of the parliamentary debate, albeit free and unrestrained, took place in a vacuum. Discussion of public issues and responsibility for their conduct remained fatefully separated from one another; hence the German people experienced an essentially distorted picture of democracy, in which parliaments were institutions where people talked almost pointlessly while action emerged from wholly different quarters. It would have been a poor beginning for a democratic experiment, even if the transition thereto had been peaceful. It was much worse under the circumstances which arose in 1918 upon the collapse of the Empire.

In World War I the control of public affairs passed from the Emperor and his inadequate aides to the Army High Command. By 1916 the Commander-in-Chief, Field Marshal Paul von Hindenburg, and even more his Chief of Staff, General Erich Ludendorff, were the actual rulers of Germany. They and the General Staff were men of high professional skill. But they knew little about the mobilization of civilians and of economic resources. The ingrained discipline of the Germans, most of whom had at one time or another been soldiers, held the country together. But this discipline rested on an unsound basis, namely the widespread ignorance over the true state of affairs. True, by the criteria which had hitherto prevailed, Germany had virtually won the war. Even on the day of the armistice not one foreign soldier stood on German soil; one major enemy, Russia, had been knocked out of the battle, and during that last year of 1918 German troops had come closer to Paris than ever before. But the generals knew that this was a last gasp of German power. When, on August 8, 1918, the "black day" of the German army, British tank forces penetrated the German line and pushed into a vacuum, even Ludendorff himself admitted in his memoir that there were no further reserves and that "the war could no longer be won."

The last Imperial Chancellor, Prince Max of Baden, was virtually forced by the High Command to negotiate an armistice with the Allies under unfavorable circumstances. But after it had been accomplished, the army chiefs denied all responsibility for it. They were aided in this astonishing maneuver by the German public, who, having been kept in ignorance throughout the war and noting that soldiers still stood deep on enemy soil, could find no rational explanation for this sudden turn of events. They saw the generals step aside and cede their places to the long-neglected politicians who now had to shoulder the thankless task of negotiating a harsh peace. The generals had lost the war, and the Emperor had fled. But in the people's minds the generals and the army remained associated with victory, while the politicians of the hastily proclaimed republic became immediately the symbols of defeat. An insidious myth, totally false in fact, but widely believed, was born: a victorious Germany was "stabbed in the back" by a conspiracy of political forces which had now taken over the country. The phrase "stab in the back" was implanted by the venerated Commander in Chief and later President of the Republic, Field Marshal Paul von Hindenburg.

Thus the infant German Republic, known from its birthplace as the Weimar Republic, became saddled from its inception with an impossible burden: that a large part of its citizens utterly rejected and despised it as a symbol of their misery and defeat. It was never to recover from this handicap.

The Weimar Constitution established a democratic and federal republic. It created a strong executive who, under certain circumstances, was able to rule by decree and suspend civil liberties in periods of emergency. But as the government was bound to have the confidence of a democratically elected parliament, such use of emergency powers was considered by the founders of the country as remote, and applicable only to exceptional periods of catastrophe or strife.

The strength of any form of government does not depend primarily on the text and the provisions of its constitution. Constitutional provisions may aid or diminish the effectiveness of a regime but, in the last analysis, they rest on political stability and political maturity. The constitutional framework of successful forms of government, notably the American and British models, has been copied by many countries throughout the world, in many cases without guaranteeing or achieving success. This was also the fate of the Weimar Republic. We have already seen that this regime was vigorously rejected, from the outset, by a substantial part of the German people. To this came the curse of a large number of political parties which fragmented the political scene. History and political experience prove that such fragmentation need not necessarily lead to the collapse of a regime; such countries as Holland and Switzerland prove that. However, when problems of exceptional gravity loom and when national unity cannot be achieved in the face of a crisis, such regimes are seriously in danger, as was later to be proven by the French Third and Fourth Republics.

Perhaps the greatest single blow to the early stability of the young Weimar Republic was the outbreak of the most fantastic inflation ever known to that day. The German government, headed by Wilhelm Cuno, wanted to improve German economic conditions before paying the reparations imposed by the Versailles Peace Treaties. But the French government of Raymond Poincaré decided to take strong measures to force the German government to pay, and occupied the heavily industrial Ruhr area. Open resistance being out of the question, passive resistance was proclaimed. This had two fateful consequences. The first was that the German government accepted short-term enlistments of volunteers who turned out to be adventurers of the worst type, many of whom played an important role in the early periods of the Hitler movement. They became known as the notorious "Black *Reichswehr*." The second and more serious consequence was that of the fiscal measures taken by the government in order to finance its campaign of passive resistance. The German government simply started to print the money it needed without protecting the value of the currency, thus causing an inflation which quickly got out of control. When this dreadful inflation came to an end in November, 1924, a new currency called *Rentenmark* was established at the incredible ratio of one new *Rentenmark* to one trillion old marks. Speculators and profiteers had a field day, but the working population was hard hit and the middle classes were financially wiped out. Henceforth embittered members of the middle class became increasingly attracted to right wing radicalism, which promised them a return to their former positions of pre-eminence once the hated "system" had been destroyed. Thus they brought to those rightist radical groups a reservoir of talent and training and even of respectability which enabled it later to come to power.

In the early years of the Weimar Republic, nationalism and anti-Republicanism were carried forward by such groups as the German Nationalist Party (*Deutsche nationale Volkspartei*), by veterans' organizations such as the "Steel Helmet," and by assorted bands of embittered and footloose ex-servicemen. Before long, a new, more radical and more militant movement began to rise, the National Socialist Workers' Party (NSDAP), frequently referred to as the Nazi Party. The world is not likely to forget it.[8]

The party's founder, Adolf Hitler, was born in Austria on the German frontier in 1889. The accident of birth made him an Austrian and he never bothered to acquire German citizenship until just before he became German Chancellor. But he always considered himself a German, and at the outbreak of World War I he chose a German rather than an Austrian regiment.

The "capital of the movement," Munich, was in those days a favorite hunting ground of all kinds of *condottieri* and adventurers. There Hitler founded, in 1919, his National Socialist

---

[8] The literature on Hitler and the Nazi regime is enormous. Still among the very best are two earlier works, Konrad Heiden, *Der Führer*, London: Gollancz, 1944 and Franz Neumann, *Behemoth: the Structure and Practice of National Socialism*, Oxford: Camden and Newforth, 1942. Very good is also Alan L. C. Bullock, *Hitler, a Study in Tyranny*, rev. ed. Harper, 1958. A popular work of almost monumental extent is William L. Shirer, *The Rise and Fall of the Third Reich, a History of Nazi Germany*, New York: Simon and Shuster, 1960.

Workers' Party. The only concrete point in that party's program was anti-Semitism; otherwise its platform was composed of vague and semi-mystical phrases.[9] The emotionalism of Hitler's appeal found ready adherents, which deceived the party's leaders into believing that the time had already come for them to take power. In 1923 Hitler staged his famous "Beerhall *Putsch*" which ended in dismal failure but which presented the movement with its first martyrs. Hitler received a short term of imprisonment in a fortress where he wrote his wellknown book *Mein Kampf*, which became the bible of the Nazi movement and its "Third Reich." The failure of the *putsch* taught Hitler the valuable lesson that it was unwise to challenge the authority of the state head on. Henceforth he was determined to come to power, not perhaps without violence, but not by direct revolutionary action either.

Nationalism, anti-Semitism (which some called Idiot's Socialism because many primitive minds thought all Jews to be capitalists and vice-versa), and the exploitation of every economic grievance, marked Nazi propaganda. The inflation and the later economic depression which created millions of desperate men and women greatly helped the movement. The skillful exploitation of the stab-in-the-back legend brought to Naziism, sooner or later, all those who had felt cheated and betrayed in 1918.

But Hitler's chief aid was without doubt his own demonic personality. He was a man with little formal education, with very partial and warped knowledge of history, with piercing black eyes and a rasping, shouting voice. His speeches, when read in print, not only lacked distinction, but in most instances were composed of single sentences and slogans thrown about without much meaning or apparent purpose. But when met in the flesh, so to speak, in a mass meeting, the same speech became a spellbinder whose hypnotic power was heightened by a skillful use of uniforms, of masses, and of martial music. Germany was a country with grievances and Hitler made it appear that he and his party were the only ones really determined to do something about them.

Already in 1924, only a year after the disastrous Beerhall

9 Apart from Hitler's *Mein Kampf* the Nazi Party's principal program was found in Gottfried Feder's *Twenty-Five Points*, written in 1920 (Munich: Eher).

Putsch flop, the Nazi party polled nearly two million votes. It was the year the great inflation reached its peak. By 1928 economic conditions had greatly improved, and the Nazi vote went down to 800,000. But the German government could not master the growing difficulties at home and abroad.

In 1930 a government was formed under Center Party leader Heinrich Bruening, a man of energy and dedication. But as the basis of his coalition government became narrower, and because he faced increasing opposition, he relied ever more heavily on the emergency provisions of the Constitution when he could not get his bills enacted through the ordinary processes of legislation. Thus the normal democratic process was already in abeyance before the Nazis came to power. When the German Parliament demanded the revocation of Bruening's emergency decrees, he prevailed upon the senile President, old Marshal Hindenburg, to call for general elections.

The elections came at the worst possible moment, however, at the height of the economic depression, and they were disastrous. While Bruening's Center Party held its own, all the other moderate parties lost heavily. The beneficiaries were the extremists. The Communists increased their vote by 40 percent, polling over 4½ million votes. The Nazis made the most spectacular gains. From their 1928 low of 800,000, they jumped to 6,400,-000 votes.

From then on, orderly parliamentary work became impossible. The sessions of the Reichstag became scenes of violence and disorder, and the government ruled by presidential decree. The democratic parties made one last major effort in March, 1932. Reich President Hindenburg was up for re-election, and this time he was the candidate of the moderates.[10] He piled up the impressive total of 18,661,736 votes compared to Hitler's 11,338,571, but he failed by less than 1 percent to carry an absolute majority, so a run-off election had to be held on April 10. This boosted

---

[10] Hindenburg was not a candidate in the first presidential election of March 29, 1925. As no candidate received a majority, a second election was called for April 26, 1925. Hindenburg, now the candidate of the right, was elected with 14,655,766 votes against the centrist Marx, the candidate of the center left parties who obtained 13,751,615 votes. 1,931,151 voted for Communist Thaelmann.

his total to well over 19,000,000 votes, while Hitler's rose to over 13,000,000. Hindenburg was elected, but the Nazi total was, nevertheless, very impressive. Bruening, who had worked hard for Hindenburg's re-election, fell victim to the intrigues of the cliques around the ailing president. He was succeeded by a renegade Centrist, Franz von Papen, who removed the constitutional government of Prussia that was dominated by the Social Democrats, and thus in effect dropped the last vestiges of democracy. If this sacrificial offering was to stop the Nazi flood and save Papen's political life, it failed to accomplish its purpose. The Nazis became the strongest party in Germany, and the Communists gained considerably at the expense of the Social Democrats and other moderate parties.

However, internal dissensions within the Nazi Party inflicted a temporary setback on Hitler when another election was called on December 3, 1932, and the Nazis lost 2,000,000 votes. In those last days of the Weimar Republic, the German scene acquired something of an unreal air, a mad dance macabre. Papen fell and was replaced by an ambitious general, Kurt von Schleicher, who headed the ambitious clique around Hindenburg. For a moment it seemed he might succeed because the Nazis were also rent by dissension. But Hitler, in contrast to his witless opponents, threw all his resources into a relatively minor election, and his success therein gave him the momentum to overcome the centrifugal tendencies in his own party. Schleicher's position deteriorated, Papen exerted his entire influence with Hindenburg and recommended that Hitler be appointed Chancellor. Hitler took office on January 30, 1933, heading a government which contained only two other Nazis beside himself, Hermann Goering (Minister for Air and Prussian Prime Minister), and Wilhelm Frick (Minister of the Interior). But if Papen and some of the Nationalists had thought that they could control Hitler, they were very much mistaken. The burning of the *Reichstag* furnished Hitler a pretext to invoke emergency decrees abolishing civil liberties and starting the Nazi terror in earnest. Until recently it had been taken for granted that the Nazis, especially Hermann Goering, had set fire to the Reichstag building. Recently discovered evidence casts some doubt on this theory, but it doesn't matter. Hitler profited to the fullest from the event and used it as an excuse to abolish the last vestiges of the legal protection of individuals.

Considering that this terror held unprecedented degrees of brutality, that mass arrests had already taken place, and that the first concentration camps had been opened, those Germans who still dared oppose Hitler deserve real credit. The last elections of the German Republic took place on March 5, 1933. Despite open intimidation and terror, the Nazis obtained only 43.9 percent of the vote, and only together with the Nationalists did they have a bare majority of 51.9 percent. They quickly swept aside these "formalities." On March 24, 1933, the Reichstag, many of whose members were already in prison, voted an enabling act transferring the entire legislative power of Parliament to Hitler. Nor was this all. When, in June, 1934, Hitler conducted a bloody purge of his own ranks, he also proclaimed himself the "Supreme Lord Justice" (Oberster Gerichtsherr) of the German people. Quickly everything was centralized, Germany was deprived of the last remaining features of federalism and took on all the aspects properly associated with a totalitarian dictatorship. Towards the end of the regime, attempts were made to fuse the machinery of the Nazi Party with that of the government, but full execution thereof was prevented by the collapse of the regime.

The Nazi regime, which had been so bombastically proclaimed as the "thousand year realm," lasted only twelve years, but it left behind it a path of death and destruction that has few equals in the history of the world. The frightening establishment of the Gestapo (Secret State Police) and of such notorious concentration camps as Dachau, Buchenwald, Ravensbruck, Bergen-Belsen, Maidanek, Oswiecim (Auschwitz), and many others remain horrible proof of the depth of depravity to which man may descend. In the terrible statistics of mass murder, the Communist regime under Stalin probably killed even more victims, but the total irrationality and incongruity of the Nazi atrocities will find few parallels. Six million Jews and millions of others were slaughtered on the basis of a hairbrained racial theory that lacked the slightest scientific evidence or basis. Innocent men and women were declared enemies of the regime. The concept of a master race was proclaimed as holy writ although denied by every act the regime committed.

It will never be possible to state accurately to what extent this nightmarish insanity was supported by the German people. As we have seen, even as late as 1932 a considerable majority of the Germans voted against Hitler. And even during the 1933 terror election, when the prisons and the torture cellars of the Gestapo were already filled, Hitler failed to obtain a majority, although not by much. It may perhaps be assumed that by 1937 or 1938 a majority of the German people did support Hitler. But some blame at least must fall on those leaders of the West whose weakness permitted Hitler to celebrate unresisted triumphs up to and including the rape of Czechoslovakia in 1939.

No responsible German can morally deny that a heavy German responsibility exists. The postwar German government of Chancellor Adenauer adopted laws for the compensation of victims of the Nazi terror and for sizable payments to the state of Israel as a form of atonement for acts, for which the German government thus accepted moral responsibility for Germany. But justice also commands us to state that once the Nazi regime was in power, active acts of resistance were extremely perilous and could be dared only by the bravest of the brave. No party, no movement, including the Communists (who have experience in such matters) can claim to have organized successful underground movements. Moreover, although the world seemed to become cognizant of the concentration camps only in 1945, or at any rate in 1939, they had existed since 1933 and most of their inmates, at least during the first five years, were Germans. Qualified observers, such as Mr. Allen Dulles and Professor Hans Rothfels estimate that from 750,000 to 1,200,000 Germans went through the concentration camps. The files of the Gestapo contained names of 2,000,000 Germans as "suspect" persons. Political death sentences up to 1938 alone are estimated to have numbered 12,000.

A major conspiracy against Hitler erupted on July 20, 1944. It was not a grassroot rebellion—that would have been quite impossible under the eye of the Gestapo. But it was amazingly widespread. It involved many top military leaders and politicians of the Weimar period, including men from the Socialists to the Nationalists. Traces of the plot were discovered in practically every major town of Germany. In occupied Paris the conspirators even succeeded in temporarily arresting the Gestapo. But the plot failed due to a series of bizarre accidents, the worst of which was that Hitler was not killed by the bomb which Col. Klaus Werner von Stauffenberg had placed under his table. Later the conspirators were arrested, hunted down, and executed in the most barbaric fashion.

At that time and for several years thereafter it seemed to many people in the outside world that the revolt of July 20, 1944 was perhaps the result of military and nationalist elements seeing the onrushing defeat and trying to escape its consequences. The inference was that they blamed Hitler primarily for bungling the war, not for starting it. Overwhelming evidence has disproved this idea. There can be little doubt that the conspirators and some of their predecessors, like the brother and sister Scholl, were moved by high ethical ideals.[11] As Allen Dulles said, they "would have to go ahead, if they chose, not in the hope of securing better peace terms, but solely because the duty to cleanse their own house was an absolute one. It was not conditional upon the help and promises of others." One of their leaders, Major General Henning von Treschkow, before committing suicide, wrote:

Everybody will now turn upon us and cover us with abuse, but my conviction remains unshaken—we have done the right thing. Hitler is not only the archenemy of Germany, he is the archenemy of the whole world. In a few hours time I shall be before God answering for my actions and omissions, and I believe that I shall be able to defend with a good conscience what I have done in the fight against Hitler. When God once promised Abraham that he would not destroy Sodom if only ten just men could be found therein, so I hope that God may save Germany from destruction for our sake. Not one of us has a right to complain about his death. Whoever entered our circle, thereby put on the Nessus shirt of doom. A man's moral value

---

[11] Hans and Sophie Scholl, brother and sister, established a small anti-Nazi group called "White Rose" and distributed leaflets opposed to Hitler and the war. Together with another group member, Christoph Probst, they were apprehended, condemned to death and executed on February 22, 1943. They were 24 and 22 years old respectively. Probst was 23. Later that year three other members of the group, Willi Graf, Alexander Schmorell and their teacher, Professor Kurt Huber, were also executed. A surviving sister of the Scholl's, Inge Scholl, has set them a monument in a little booklet entitled *Die weisse Rose*, Frankfurt, Verlag Frankfurter Hefte. 1952.

begins only when he is prepared to sacrifice his life for his convictions.[12]

True, for every Treschkow there were several hundreds, perhaps thousands, of Anne Franks. But however unequal the numerical balance, the Treschkows, Stauffenbergs, von Hassels, Kieps, and their comrades attempted to save what could still be saved of German honor.

---

[12] Hans Speidel, *Invasion 1944*, Tübingen and Stuttgart, Wunderlich (undated) p. 146.

CHAPTER TWO

Destruction and
Rebirth

THE FAILURE of the revolt of July 20, 1944, sealed Germany's
fate in the sense that the destruction of Naziism could now be
achieved only by the military might of the Allied Powers and not
by any internal upheaval. This had two fateful consequences: it
visited enormous destruction on Germany because the greatest
concentration of air raids and invasion occurred after July, 1944,
and it also deprived Germany of any political group which could
take power when defeat struck. Hence the only feasible alternative
for Germany's immediate postwar period was military government
by the occupying powers.

This had been anticipated. A conference of foreign ministers,
meeting in Moscow in October, 1943, established the European
Advisory Commission which was charged with preparing plans
for the occupation of Germany. Later, in 1944, the provisional
government of France was invited to participate in these delibera-
tions. When the Commission was unable to produce agreement, a
decision on a higher level was called for. At the Yalta Conference
in February, 1945, President Franklin D. Roosevelt, Prime Minister Winston Churchill, and Generalissimo Josef Stalin decided
that the United States, the U.S.S.R., and Great Britain should
each occupy a zone in Germany, and that the French government should be invited to accept a similar zone for administration. It was also decided that the Soviet Union should occupy
hitherto Polish land approximately as far as the so-called Curzon
Line went, and that in turn Poland should be compensated by
"substantial accessions" of German territory. Later, the Potsdam
Conference of August, 1945, handed over to "Polish administra-

19

tion" all German territory east of the Rivers Oder and Neisse plus the city of Stettin. The northern part of East Prussia, including the city of Königsberg (renamed Kalinengrad), was ceded to the Soviet Union.

Before that, all German authority over Germany had come to an end with the unconditional surrender of May 7 and 8, 1945. The phantom government of Admiral Karl Doenitz, which had never exercised actual governmental authority, was dissolved and its members arrested.

The total obliteration of all German indigenous authority must have appeared like the harbinger of a Carthaginian peace. When this author, then an officer in the United States Army, conducted, during the closing days of the war, an informal survey of views among students and faculty of the University of Marburg, he encountered the quasi-unanimous view that Germany was finished and would never rise again as a nation. It is clear that this attitude, widespread as it was in 1945, proved quite unfounded. In actual fact Allied occupation, despite its obvious shortcomings, was beneficial in many ways and lasted for a much shorter time than was anticipated. But it did have one lasting consequence of great severity: the division of Germany.

How did it occur? Was it avoidable? After much re-examination of the facts, this author, at any rate, has come to the conclusion that the division of Germany was a great tragedy which is bound to loom ever larger, but if one looks at the data which were available during those crucial days of decision and not in the rosy light of twenty-twenty hindsight, it is difficult to see how a division could have been avoided.

In the years 1943 and 1944 the Allies had to take fateful decisions. Some agreement with the Soviet Union on the future occupation of Germany had become imperative. After the Battle of Stalingrad in January, 1943, the Soviet armies moved westward. No span of oceans separated the Russian soldiers from their German objectives. On the other hand, the great Allied invasion of the Continent was still one and a half years ahead, and an invasion of such magnitude against a formidable opponent had never been undertaken before. Its initial success was likely, but not a foregone conclusion. The speed with which the Western Allied armies were to penetrate into Germany could not be exactly foreseen. It might have been hoped that the Soviet and Western armies might meet at the Oder River, but it was just as possible that they might meet at the Rhine. Stalin had said, "without Germany we cannot win and with Germany we cannot lose." It was clear from the experiences with Russian occupations of such countries as Poland, Rumania, and Bulgaria that Stalin's grip over Germany would be unrestrained if the Russians were to manage to occupy most of that country and be unfettered by a binding agreement regarding its future administration.

Diplomats must always ask themselves, "What if I am wrong?" From the vista of 1943 and 1944 the Western Allies were bound to come to the conclusion that the absence of an occupation agreement with the Soviet Union and total reliance on Anglo-American success in occupying a larger part of Germany created the appalling risk of putting the whole of Germany in Stalin's grip in the event of a faster advance of the Soviet army than that of its Western counterpart. The consequences of such an event would have been incalculable and had to be avoided at all costs.

Now if one accepts the reality that an occupation agreement with the Soviet Union became imperative in 1943 and 1944, then the outlines of the present situation already appear.

1. Germany had to be divided and administered in several zones of occupation. A single, integrated Allied military government organization was totally out of the question. It had worked badly enough in Italy among British and American forces where no language barrier existed. In Germany neither the Russians nor the French wanted any part of a single administrative structure. The Russians, in particular, were completely adamant.

2. Zones of occupation had to be approximately equal in area, number of inhabitants and economic significance. This does not apply to the French zone which was carved out of the American and British ones.

3. The respective zones of occupation had to be as close as possible to the respective occupying power's national territory.

We have already shown why neither an all-German unified administration nor an integrated administration was possible for Germany in 1945. In this light, then, the above three rules for the designation of the zones of occupation would appear inescapable. A further look at the map will, moreover, reveal that the zones could not easily have been very different from what they were and still meet the above criteria. This also meant that the previous capital of Berlin was bound to be either in the Soviet zone or surrounded by it, being located not in the center of Germany but in its eastern part.

It is interesting to recall that both the Western and the Soviet occupation authorities began their respective tasks under assumptions which proved erroneous.

The Western Allies, especially the Americans, had elaborately prepared for their role. They had expected a very long period of occupation and military government during which not only the political but also the social structure of Germany were to be profoundly remodeled. All kinds of social theories, many of them of rather questionable veracity, were propagated, often over-simplifying the reasons for which Germany had accepted Naziism and prescribing often drastic solutions in order to avoid a recurrence. Most of these theories evaporated quickly enough in the light of practical realities.

There were, however, more fateful divisions of opinion. Within the United States government, the State and Defense Departments favored extensive decentralization and both military and economic disarmament under international control. On the other hand, a powerful but informal group, headed by the then Secretary of the Treasury, Henry Morgenthau, pressed for a disbandment of Germany. Certain British groups also favored disbandment, although they did not acquire the influence of the Morgenthau group in the United States.

In the meantime the invasion of Europe by the Western Allies became imminent and the military commanders, especially General Dwight D. Eisenhower, Commander in Chief, became concerned over the need of military government guidelines and the availability of military government teams lest the combat army were to become burdened with this task. Training and planning were therefore instituted, especially in Shrivenham, England, before a final policy on occupied Germany was decided upon. In effect the planners had to make their own rules, which followed to some extent the assumptions of both State and War Department thinking. However, Morgenthau carried his ideas directly to President Franklin D. Roosevelt and obtained the acceptance of his plan at the second Quebec conference in September, 1944. Moreover, President Roosevelt persuaded Prime Minister Winston Churchill to accept this drastic solution in principle.

Thus both the State Department and War Department policy proposals were turned down and the planning effort in Shrivenham nullified. But by that time the invasion of the Continent was underway, the armies were on the move, and the first sectors of German territory were occupied without any unified occupation policy having been settled.

The Morgenthau plan never became a reality but its attitude had an impact on official American policy. Just prior to the armistice, the first general directive for the occupation of Germany was issued by the United States Chiefs of Staff on April 26, 1945 (JCS 1067). Their guiding principles were stated in these terms:

It should be brought home to the Germans that Germany's ruthless warfare and the fanatical Nazi resistance have destroyed the German economy and have made chaos and suffering inevitable and that the Germans cannot escape responsibility for what they have brought upon themselves.

Germany will not be occupied for the purpose of liberation, but as a defeated enemy nation. . . . The principal Allied objective is to prevent Germany from ever again becoming a threat to the peace of the world. . . .

To this end, the following steps were to be taken:

1. Nothing was to be done to bring about the economic rehabilitation of Germany except insofar as it was necessary in the interests of the security of the Allied military forces.
2. No relief was to be extended to the German people except in order to avoid disease and such disorder as might impede the Allied military effort.
3. De-Nazification and demilitarization were to be carried out under all circumstances.

The almost completely negative character of these rules is striking. Nothing was said about encouraging political life of any sort. Quite evidently there was the underlying assumption not only of a very long period of military government but also of a situation in which German political life would remain indefinitely in a state of suspended animation.

The total irreality of these assumptions can only serve to make us cautious about the efficacy of human foresight and planning. Powerful political pressure and understandable human desires quickly reduced the Allied military establishment after the armistice, as officers and men were brought home and demobilized. The Military Government units did not remain immune from this manpower drain. Moreover, dispirited and stunned as the Germans were, it was nevertheless natural that many Germans who had been connected with the Weimar Republic and had somehow survived the Nazi holocaust would now come forward. Many of them were employed by the military government to man the innumerable administrative posts which had to be filled. Other Germans who either had no political past or even who had a highly questionable one which they managed to hide, also offered their services.

To be sure, the Allied authorities, having the totality of physical power in their hands, were in effect in a position to suppress the slightest stirring of political life. The text of the Joint Chiefs of Staff Directive would have demanded that. But in effect the local and regional military government officers were far too dependent on German help to suppress drastically all stirrings of political rebirth. The problems of transportation, of food, of water, of epidemic control, of housing, and many others, overshadowed all political directives. Moreover, only utterly ruthless acts of repression could have stamped out these early political stirrings. Such drastic action lay neither within Western political mores, nor in the sentiments of the United States, British, and French officers involved.

The negative aspects of these directives showed their complete inapplicability, and they quickly became a dead letter. However, their existence had prevented a positive Allied policy from emerging, and thus different approaches were noticeable not only in the three Western zones of occupation but even within each zone between cities and regions. Nevertheless, the devoted and in many cases effective work of individual Military Government teams and their German assistants should not be discounted. But of an over-all policy, there existed very little.

Perhaps one of the thorniest problems was that of de-Nazification. The brutality of the Nazi regime had become known to all the world. Americans in particular had been slow to accept the facts of concentration camps, torture, and extermination, and the discoveries of such infernos as Dachau, Buchenwald, and Bergen-Belsen came as a great psychological shock. Clearly something had to be done to purge Germany of those who had committed such crimes. This determination prevailed particularly among American policy makers. What defeated it in the end was not the concept of de-Nazification itself but that the concept was applied with excessive ambition. There was nothing in itself wrong with this ambition; what was wrong was that the number of people who were to be screened and judged became too great to be processed by the available manpower of the courts and commissions established for that purpose.

Initially it had been the policy of the United States to decree automatic arrest and ineligibility for office of any kind to all holders of certain ranks in Nazi party organizations. Party membership was cause for ineligibility for all but menial jobs, if membership antedated 1937.[1] The application of these rules created conditions contrary to well-established principles of Anglo-American justice because they created a presumption of guilt until proven innocent, while the slow grinding of the courts provided for long periods of imprisonment without trial. Nevertheless the de-Nazification system in itself was not intrinsically unfair. What made it so was the number of cases involved. In the American zone alone, over 11,000,000 people had to register. No authorities existed, American or German, which could handle such a staggering number with any degree of expedition.

Eventually, responsibility for screening and trial had to be turned over to German authorities. A "Law for the Liberation from National Socialism and Militarism" was finally proclaimed by the Council of Prime Ministers of the American zone, and approved by military government on March 25, 1946. It established five classes of persons required to register as Nazis depending on the gravity of their offenses and associations. But there was friction between the German and American authorities over

[1] In 1937 the German Civil Service Code was enacted and great pressure was exerted against civil servants to join the Nazi Party.

the question of whether people should be tried and screened out merely for positions held, or only for actual crimes committed. By the end of 1946, the untenable character of procedure became obvious as, after nine months of the law's operation, only a little over 1 percent of those who had registered had been tried or otherwise processed. So many people lived under the shadow of future prosecution that there was danger of their becoming a problem to public safety. Eventually, in July, 1946, military government granted an amnesty to certain categories of Germans, which was extended to other groups by the end of that year. But because of the large number of cases and the general impatience to get the business over with, de-Nazification became more and more a mechanical process and increasing leniency set in in the disposition of cases.

This in itself fostered an injustice, because in many cases, lesser offenders had been tried first while more serious cases were expected to "stew in their own juice" until their time would come. In effect, that meant that many lesser offenders were tried under stringent interpretations of the rules which more serious offenders came up after a policy of greater leniency had set in.

The experience with de-Nazification in the American zone has been generally judged as highly unsatisfactory. But at least a serious attempt was made there to tackle the problem. The British had a brief try, though on the whole confined themselves to grave cases. In the French and Soviet zones there never was any real de-Nazification to speak of, although some former Nazi leaders were liquidated with or without trial. In July, 1947, Marshal Sokolovsky declared a virtual amnesty for all Nazis in the Soviet zone except for the most serious offenders. Former Nazis who joined the Communist-dominated principal government party were treated with indulgence and often with considerable favor, as their past records put them at the mercy of the Soviet authorities. Frequently they were preferred over less pliable men of proven anti-Nazi convictions.

The isolation of the American de-Nazification effort, the tremendous scope of the task, the many inner conflicts over policy, both within the American elements and between it and the Germans, all contributed to deprive the program of much of its original meaning. But had it not been attempted, the suspicion that Germany had remained unregenerated would have remained strong. Thus, despite its failures and shortcomings, the isolated and fruitless but massive American and German efforts in the American zone did have some beneficial consequences for the new German state.

In the Western zones the failures and shortcomings of occupation policy were the result of the already mentioned fundamental concepts both of the duration and of the military occupation, as well as of the realities of political life.

The failures of military government policy in the Soviet zone stemmed from a different origin. Soviet military forces had no specific military government organization, and vested responsibility in their respective commanders of combat units who had the help—if help it was—of the commissars and the secret police. Because the Communists always gave priority to political considerations, the Russians from the start relied heavily on German Communists, many of whom had sought refuge in the Soviet Union and had been brought back by the Soviet army. Chief among them were two old line Communists, Wilhelm Pieck and Walter Ulbricht. Other German groups which the Russians attempted to use were the "Free Germany Committee" and the "Union of German Officers" founded among German prisoners of war, especially from the army of Field Marshal Friedrich von Paulus which had surrendered at Stalingrad.

In addition to the use of these individuals and groups, the Russians embarked on an occupation policy which in its early phase contrasted sharply with that of the Western Allies. While the latter, especially the Americans, went heavily into de-Nazification procedures, the Russians, as we have seen, gave them only a perfunctory brush. While in the Western zones, schools, theaters and the like were only slowly and gradually opened as de-Nazification caught up with the work, they were opened immediately in the Russian zone. Most important of all, the Russians immediately licensed four political parties in their zone while the Western powers had forbidden all political activities until they could see clearly whom they could trust. Thus the odd situation occurred that the Russians, whose severity had been so greatly feared by the Germans, were at first more liberal in the application of occupation policies than the Western

powers, whose tradition would have tended to make them more
lenient.

One might speculate whether these often quite enlightened
Soviet policies might not have achieved the results desired by
the Soviet authorities had the conduct of the Russian soldiers
not been so abominable as to nullify their effect. But in a curious way Russian policies had a profound effect—on the Western
occupied zones. The decision by the Soviet military authorities
to license political parties greatly accelerated the pace with which
political parties were permitted to organize in the West, and
once the Western powers decided to act in accordance with
their own traditions and proven institutions, they entered into a
type of competition with the Russians which the latter could
not possibly win.

In licensing four political parties the Soviet occupation authorities sought to accomplish two objectives: (1) German memories
of the Weimar Republic underscored in particular the galaxy of
parties which had been responsible for at least a good part of
that regime's chronic instability. By limiting the parties to four,
the Russians countered this fear. (2) As we have already shown,
they stole a march on the Western Allies by proceeding almost
immediately with the re-creation of political life. However, this
policy failed to achieve the Russian objectives. And the new
political parties showed evidence of wishing to remain independent. It was the Social Democratic Party, which had always
had its greatest strength in Eastern Germany, that proved a
particularly hard nut to crack. Under the leadership of Dr. Kurt
Schumacher, the party established its national seat in West Germany and defied the Russians. It soon became clear that party
discipline was very strong among the Social Democrats and that
there was little sympathy for common cause with the Communists.

When the Russians realized that their policy, however shrewd,
had misfired, they increasingly abandoned the velvet glove and
showed the iron fist. Great pressure was directed against the
Social Democratic leaders to fuse their party with the much
smaller Communist Party. The rank and file resisted vigorously
but in Eastern Germany some Social Democratic leaders were
found who, for one reason or another, decided to throw in

with the Communists. Chief among them was Otto Grotewohl who defied Schumacher's injunction against making common cause with the Communists. Throughout the Soviet zone the Russians quickly suppressed meetings at which the rank and file of the Social Democratic Party could voice their opposition against their renegade leaders. In East Berlin, however, due to the then still existent quadripartite Allied control, such meetings could not be suppressed, and the rank and file party membership voted down the Communist fusion propaganda by an overwhelming majority of seven to one. Nevertheless, Grotewohl and his cohorts went ahead and in June, 1946, the fusion of the two parties was forcefully accomplished. The new united party gave itself the name of Socialist Unity Party of Germany *(Sozialistische Einheitspartei Deutschlands)* commonly referred to as the SED. As in all such cases the Social Democrats were permitted to provide members while the Communists provided the control.

One more contest remained possible. On October 20, 1946, elections were held throughout Berlin, both East and West, and due to Allied control, they were free. Both the Social Democratic Party (SPD) and the SED were able to run candidates in all four sectors of the city and so did the other parties. The SED went into this contest with high hopes; not only did it enjoy the wholehearted support of the Soviet authorities but it also counted on the "red" tradition of Berlin, a city in which the Nazis had never been able to obtain a majority. The voters, however, handed the Socialist Unity Party a resounding defeat. Of 1,945,981 votes cast, the SED obtained only 383,249, or slightly less than 20 percent. Strongest remained the old line Social Democratic Party which polled 948,851, or just under 49 percent. The Christian Democratic Union, a middle of the road to conservative party, occupied second place with 432,016 votes or 22 percent, while the right wing Liberal Democratic Party was last with 181,875 or a little over 9 percent. Even in the Soviet sector of Berlin the SED obtained only 29.8 percent of the vote while the SPD garnered 43.6 percent.

The elections were a turning point for they proved conclusively to the Russians that by no cleverness of policy could they obtain German adherents. If they wanted control, they had to acquire it by force. From that time on the regime became harsher, while political opponents were suppressed with increasing ruthlessness and ever-increasing numbers. Russian-occupied Germany became the most satellite of all satellite countries and, although Grotewohl remained a figurehead Prime Minister until his death in 1964, actual power was wielded by the universally detested Communist leader Walter Ulbricht. The dream of the Communists of making East Germany a springboard from which to penetrate and conquer West Germany, had vanished. To keep control of East Germany, the Communists were now forced to turn it into a fully Communist state. It was this act which finalized the division of Germany. Now the quadripartite Allied control commission for Germany, as well as its Berlin replica the *Kommandantura*, quickly lost their significance as the Russians first sabotaged the proceedings, and then walked out.

The division of Germany had been neither the policy of the West nor that of the Soviet Union; but to Russia it became a second line of retreat after the dream of dominating Germany as a whole had definitely foundered.

CHAPTER THREE

Once More a State

IT WOULD BE difficult to view the period of Allied military occupation of Germany without very mixed feelings. In retrospect, certainly, many policies and endeavors must seem highly unrealistic. Perhaps most of the more fantastic concepts had their origin in the naive belief that somehow the political evolution of Germany would stand still until the occupiers in their omnipotence would permit the wheel to turn another notch. Among some Americans, some highly theoretical ideas about the possibilities and desirability of a wholesale restructuring of German society were also current. In the British zone an extraordinary attempt was made to transplant the English system of local government into the wholly different conditions and traditions of Germany; the French would have been just as happy not to have any German government at all beyond the Laender level. Their aspirations were in some respects more practical and of a short term nature, as they were second only to the Russians in removing goods and equipment from Germany in the understandable desire to rebuild their own ravaged country. The French also hoped to permanently detach the Saarland from Germany, a project for which they would evidently need some time.

Perhaps one of the lessons of this very interesting period is that the degree to which even an omnipotent foreign government can affect wholesale structural changes is more limited than many had thought.

Yet it would be highly unfair to look upon the Western Allied occupation of Germany in an altogether negative light. Despite numerous shortcomings and errors, the occupation was on the whole exceedingly benign. Historians will find it difficult to uncover other examples where the occupation authorities of a recent enemy had tried so genuinely, and often at considerable sacrifice, to lighten the desolation and despair of their charges. And that was done despite necessity for the increasingly important American economic aid which eventually reached gigantic proportions.[1] In fact, considering the total disorganization of Germany at the end of hostilities, the absence of usable German authorities, and the political impossibility of permitting the continued existence of the civil service and other structures and personnel without some purification, it is difficult to see how there could have been the rebirth of Germany under its present constitutional structure without an intermediary phase of military government.

The Soviet zone of occupation was quickly turned into a Communist satellite regime and shall not be further considered here. But even the three Allied zones of occupation pursued quite different policies. In many respects the American zone proved most successful and its methods of administration have had more long-lasting effect. This was not only due to the greater generosity with which the United States aided this process, but, even more, was the result of America's own federal tradition which came closer to an older German tradition and to the desire of German administrators and political leaders than was the case in the British and French zones. Also, the American occupation personnel, being far from home and its prosperous post-war economy to which they were eager to return, were most anxious to put German administration on its feet. In this spirit the American authorities were more inclined to permit the Laender governments to exercise powers of central governments especially in Bavaria. Moreover, under the inspiration and guidance of a noted American political scientist, Professor James K. Pollock, a Council of States (*Laenderrat*) was established at Stuttgart, consisting of the minister presidents of the Laender in the American zone (including the Mayors of Hamburg and Bremen) with their staffs. A prominent secretariat with sub-committees for major economic and technical problems prepared the ground for certain zonewide administrative organisms, for coordination of planning

---

[1] United States economic aid to Germany from July 1, 1945 to December 31, 1959 amounted to $3,900,000,000 not counting the large scale private assistance which came through numerous individuals as well as religious and other American organizations, such as CARE. By comparison American aid during the above period to Great Britain amounted to $7,000,-000,000 and to France, $5,500,000,000.

and administration between the Laender, and thus set the stage for later developments.

British planning was, in some respects, more ambitious and perhaps less realistic than the American counterpart but provided efficient and capable administration, although with more reluctance than their American colleagues to turn jurisdiction over to German authorities. In this respect the French were even more reluctant. The policies of the occupation authorities were sufficiently divergent that a unified approach to the re-establishment of a German governmental structure might have been quite difficult had it not been for the intervention of extraneous factors.

The rapidly deteriorating East-West relations, and the manner in which the Soviet zone of Germany was turned into a satellite regime, made it clear that the provisions of the Potsdam Agreement according to which "during the period of occupation, Germany shall be treated as a single economic unit" (item 14) and the central administrative departments envisaged therein (item 9, IV), would never come into realization. At the same time it was obvious that the Laender were too small to become the exclusive or even the major units of government. Confronted by a dangerous stagnation and decline of whatever was left of the German economy, the Western powers were obliged to undertake such combinations as were available to them. We have already mentioned the Council of Laender in the American zone. Since September, 1946, a progressive fusion of functions in the British and American zones had taken place. This showed many shortcomings and needed several revisions.

Therefore in June, 1948, in London, a conference in which the United States, Great Britain, France, Belgium, the Netherlands, and Luxembourg were represented, provided for (a) the eventual fusion of the three western zones, (b) the establishment of a provisional West German government, (c) an occupation statute which was to define the powers of the occupying countries and of Germany respectively, (d) an international authority of the Ruhr, and (e) minor territorial adjustments of Germany's western frontier.

On July 1, 1948, the prime ministers of the eleven Laender comprising the Western zones were summoned to Frankfurt to be officially notified of the decisions of the London Conference.

They were told of the numerous rights which the occupation authorities still intended to reserve unto themselves and also were authorized to convene not later than September 1, 1948 and to constitute an assembly composed of delegates chosen by the various *Land* parliaments in proportion to the size of the respective Laender populations.

The result was a pandemonium. Perhaps the rapid transition from total submission under military government to the formulation of a constituent act was too great. Some less responsible party leaders even went so far as to see in the inevitable shortages and privations of the immediate post-war period a deliberate Allied policy to bend the Germans to their will. More serious were the objections to the drafting of a constitutional document when so many far-reaching rights were reserved to the uncontrolled authority of the Allied powers. How was one to draft and make credible the ground rules for a democratic government when many vital rights were removed from the normal political, legal, and judicial restraints of a democratic constitution? Would those who participated in the drafting of a constitution under conditions of this kind not later be denounced as the servile campfollowers of alien authorities?

But most serious of all was the widespread concern lest the drafting of a constitution for West Germany would fatally compromise Germany's eventual reunification since it might be interpreted as a definitive recognition of Germany's division.

There were some temperamental outbursts on both sides but reason eventually prevailed. A major battle was also fought over the occupation statute. The German objections were numerous, but few of them were permitted to survive. On September 21, 1949 the Occupation Statute entered into force substantially as agreed upon by the three Western foreign ministers at the Washington Conference of April, 1949. The restrictions imposed on the Germans by the Occupation Statute were so extensive that their unwise use could have seriously militated against any German constitution being taken seriously. However, the Allies showed commendable restraint in the exercise of their powers, which were rapidly limited, first by the Petersburg Protocol of November 22, 1949, and then by the first treaty to which post-war Germany was again a party. It was signed on May 26, 1952, by the Foreign Ministers of Britain, France, and the United States, as well as by the Chancellor of the new German Federal Republic. This treaty restored almost complete sovereignty to Germany, revoked the Occupation Statute, abolished the Allied High Commission, and the offices of the *Land* Commissioners. This treaty was dependent upon the ratification of the so-called European Defense Community. After the European Defense Community Treaty was defeated in the French National Assembly in 1954, the Bonn Treaty text was incorporated into a new agreement called the Treaty to Establish a Western European Union. The Allied High Commissioners who, upon the adoption of the German Constitution in 1949, had replaced the military governments, were transformed into ambassadors in June, 1953. The New Germany, the German Federal Republic (*Deutsche Bundesrepublik*) was now a fully sovereign power.[2]

We have seen earlier that one of the principal preoccupations of the members of the parliamentary council which drafted the new German Constitution was the fear that any such document might recognize as permanent the division of Germany. This was accommodated by using the term "basic law" (*Grundgesetz*) rather than the more traditional word "constitution" (*Verfassung*) as the official designation of this document, although the legal difference between those two terms is scarcely visible to the naked eye. But the term "basic law" does, at least semantically, connote a less prominent and "constitutive" document than the word "constitution."

This thought was more clearly expressed in the preamble to the "basic law" which proclaimed that it was that document's purpose "to give a new order to political life for a *transitional* period."* The same preamble also called upon "the entire German people to achieve, by free self-determination, the unity and freedom of Germany." For the transitional period during which this freedom was obviously denied to the people in the Soviet-occupied zone, the preamble further stated that those who es-

---

[2] The International Authority of the Ruhr was established on December 28, 1948 but never reached full effectiveness. With the establishment of the European Coal and Steel Authority (Schuman Plan), the Ruhr Authority was officially terminated in February 1953.

* Author's italics.

tablished this basic document had "also acted on behalf of those Germans to whom participation was denied." With this wording, the authors of the Constitution managed at one and the same time to refuse recognition to Germany's division, to proclaim the transitional character of the German Federal Republic, and to proclaim its right to speak for the whole of Germany until Germany could again be reunified in freedom. It could be said, therefore, that this document recognized the eventual dissolution of the present German Federal Republic into a reunified Germany.

CHAPTER FOUR

Political Life

GERMANY has had some sort of parliamentary life for somewhat over one hundred years. In that period numerous political parties have come and gone. Only two have persisted, the Social Democratic Party on the moderate left, and a Christian Party of the moderate right which, until 1933, was Catholic and called *Zentrum* (Center Party). It was reborn on an interdenominational basis after World War II under the name of Christian Democratic Union.

The origins and the aspirations of the two parties were different, yet they had certain features in common which have marked their mutual relationship. Both were persecuted by Bismarck and yet emerged victorious from the struggle. Both inherited the heavy burden of creating and governing the Weimar Republic and, therefore both came in for the bitter attacks of the Nationalists and the Nazis. Theirs has been a fateful relationship both as partners and as antagonists.

Here again, a brief glimpse of the historical background of Germany's political parties is essential to an understanding of their present activities, positions, strengths, and of public attitudes toward them.

A Catholic parliamentary group was first created in the Prussian Diet in 1852 in opposition to certain anti-Catholic measures of the Minister of Culture. The fact that his ministerial edicts were clearly in contravention of the Prussian constitution started this Catholic group out as the defender of legality and parliamentary control. Similar developments took place in the other German states. This group came to call itself the "Group of the Center" (*Fraktion des Zentrums*) after the place its members occupied in the Parliament, and also in order to indicate that it was not irrevocably opposed to the government, as was the left.

The Center Party was formally founded in anticipation of the elections to the Prussian parliament of 1870 and under this title it also entered the new parliament of the Second Reich. The minority position of Catholics in Prussia, and even more so in the North German Federation, and then the German Reich, coincided with developments in the Catholic Church, such as the declaration of the infallibility of the Pope, which tended to sharpen the contrast between Catholics and Protestants. It was only natural for the Center to seek contacts with other minority groups, the Poles, the Guelphs, and the Alsatians,[1] and to try and work with other parties opposed to the government. This brought members of the Center into sharp conflict with Bismarck but also made them firm defenders of the constitutional order and of democracy.

The Social Democratic Party of Germany (SPD) had a different origin. It arose as a part of the international Socialist movement and was from its outset strongly influenced by the theories of Karl Marx and Friedrich Engels. Originally it was split into several movements, notably the General German Workers' Association headed by Ferdinand Lasalle, and a more Marxist movement headed by August Bebel and Wilhelm Liebknecht. The two movements were united at the Party convention of Gotha in 1875 on the basis of a Marxist program but in the spirit of democracy. The decision that the struggle for power would be conducted only by legal means excluded revolution.

The Party was just getting well underway when Bismarck's anti-Socialist laws struck it in 1878. As has been said before, by modern standards of dictatorship and suppression, these laws were quite mild. The Party remained in existence despite considerable inconveniences, pressures, and arrests. Throughout the twelve years of the law's operation, the Party was able to have its candidates run for office although under often quite disadvantageous circumstances. The end of the laws made it possible for the Social Democratic Party to develop to the fullest and when

---

[1] The partitions of Poland (1772, 1793, 1795, 1815) had placed a part of Poland under Prussian rule. The Guelfs (*Welfen*) were the adherents of the Hanoverian dynasty who resented Hanover's incorporation into Prussia. Alsace and a part of Lorraine came to Germany in 1871.

World War I began, it was the strongest party in the old Reichstag. Thus both the Social Democrats and the Center Party had profited from Bismarck's persecution and had become the most important parliamentary groups. Their common experiences had made both of them defenders of the constitutional and parliamentary order. But in imperial Germany this did not bring them even one step closer to governmental responsibility because the government was responsible not to parliament, but to the Emperor alone. Consequently, neither party obtained experience in the actual conduct of government until it was suddenly, overnight, thrust upon them under the worst possible circumstances.

The outbreak of World War I not only stopped all discriminatory measures of the government against both the Center and the Social Democratic Parties, but in turn caused them to support the German war effort. There was actually no *quid pro quo* involved in this. The German government desired German unity to round out the picture and the reality of "a nation in arms." That the Center Party supported the war effort was not surprising. It was perhaps less natural for the Social Democratic Party, nominally Marxist, whose theories had once decreed that in the event of war the workers of the warring nations would find that they had more in common with one another than with their masters. This theory collapsed thoroughly, not only in Germany, but in the other belligerent countries as well. Of great importance was also the fact that for Germany the first enemy was Russia, which in the thinking of the German workers epitomized blackest reaction and the mortal enemy of socialism in Europe. Certainly too, there was the natural feeling of national solidarity in the face of external danger. As said before, one must remember that the German system of government in 1914 with all its imperfections and limitations could not even remotely be compared to the oppressive tyranny of the Hitler regime in 1939.

World War I brought about important changes. The time when the government could do as it pleased, regardless of Parliament, came to an end. Chancellor Georg Michaelis was the first to realize that he could not govern without the confidence of a parliamentary majority, and his successor Karl, Count von Hertling, was the first Chancellor-designate to confer with the majority parties and to assure himself of their support before accepting the office. The Center Party remained united throughout the war. The Social Democrats did not. Their left wing, led by Karl Liebknecht and Rosa Luxembourg, entered into opposition against the Party leadership and against the war effort. Nevertheless, the majority of the Party remained intact and at the very end of the war the Social Democrats joined with the Center Party and others in entering a government for the first time, that of Prince Max von Baden.

When the loss of the war became known—for it became known only at the very end—the regime inevitably became the target in the search for culprits as the Emperor fled to the Netherlands.

We have already seen how the Social Democrats and the Center Party were forced by circumstances to take over the government of Germany in the hour of defeat and collapse. In the years to come, they became the target of those nationalists who were only too glad to transfer the guilt for the lost war from those who had perpetrated, led, and lost it, to the democratic parties of the Weimar Republic. Both the Center Party and the Social Democrats, especially the latter, suffered cruelly under the unjust accusation that they had been lacking in national devotion and that they had betrayed their country. This was to have an important impact on their thinking when they returned to active political life after the downfall of the Hitler regime.

All political parties were outlawed by Hitler in 1933 and their leaders persecuted, imprisoned, or killed unless they were able to escape abroad. Practically the entire slate of the top leadership of both parties disappeared, from natural or unnatural causes, during the Nazi period. The only one who survived, former Center Party Chancellor Heinrich Bruening, had become exceedingly controversial and did not find it opportune to return to Germany permanently. Thus both parties returned to political life after 1945 with leaders who had either been of the second string during the Weimar Republic, or who were unknown. As it turned out, this did not handicap them greatly.

At first the initial attempts of political leaders to recreate their organizations did not meet with an enthusiastic response. For the twelve years of the Nazi regime the people had been over-politicized; all questions, even of the most personal concern, had been surrounded by the Nazi regime with political significance. Now there was a reaction. In general the German people were bitter, apathetic, hungry and tired. Furthermore, Allied military government policy outlawed political activities in the beginning; later, political activity was gradually permitted at the simplest level, and without license for a party press.

As previously related, the Soviets did not have the elaborate military government setup of the Western Allics and preferred to rely instead on German Communists and on their own political skill. Hence, the Russians were much faster in licensing zone-wide political parties, but at the same time permitted only a reduced number of them to exist. When the Russians saw that their initial liberality did not advance their aims, they quickly discarded this system, making way for an outright Communist dictatorship. In thc Western zones, however, the Soviet initiative helped speed up the admission of political parties to active political life and remind Germans and Allies alike of the undesirability of returning to the galaxy of political parties which characterized the Weimar regime. Out of this arose the present situation in which three political parties have survived with one of them, however, almost certainly on the decline, thus opening the path to an eventual two-party system in Germany.

The Christian Democrats

The contemporary Christian Democratic Union (CDU) and its Bavarian sister-party, the Christian Social Union (CSU) follow in their political theory and their programs the pattern laid down by other Christian Democratic Parties in Europe, such as the French Popular Republican Movement (MRP). They place Christian ethics in the center of their outlook and they accept the principle that the freedom of the will which is so important to Christian thinking must be safeguarded not only in the philosophical and ethical realm but also in the political, economic, and social. But beyond these very general principles, the fortunes of the CDU/CSU have been quite different from those of the French MRP. They have also been different and distinct from those of the old Center Party, the spiritual father of the CDU/CSU.

Votes and Seats in the Bundestag of Major Parties

Parties	1949		1953			1957			1961			1965		
	Percent of vote	Seats	Percent of vote	Seats		Percent of vote	Seats		Percent of vote	Seats		Vote	Percent of vote	Seats[a]
CDU/CSU	31.0	139	45.2	244		50.2	270		45.4	242		15,392,973	47.6	245
SPD	29.2	131	28.8	151		31.8	169		36.2	190		12,711,726	39.3	202
FDP	11.9	52	9.5	48		7.7	41		12.8	67		3,062,948	9.5	49
GB-BHE			5.9	27		4.6	—		} 2.8 {	} — {				
DP	4.0	17	3.3	15		3.4	17		} {	} {		[b]	3.6	
KPD	5.7	15	2.2	—										

[a] The nonvoting seats from Berlin are not listed.
[b] All splinter parties together. None of them received seats in the *Bundestag* under the 5%-minimum clause.
They were:

AUD (*Aktionsgemeinschaft unabhaengiger Deutschen*—Action group of independent Germans) 52,688 votes, 0.2% of total.
CVP (*Christliche Volkspartei*—Christian People's party) 19,904 votes, 0.1% of total.
DFU (*Deutsche Friedensunion*—German Peace Union) 432,221 votes, 1.3% of total.
FSU (*Freisoziale Union*—Free Social Union) 10,763 votes, 0.0% of total.
NPD (*Nationaldemokratische Partei Deutschlands*—National Democratic Party of Germany) 658,250 votes, 2.0% of total.

The CVP is confined to the Saarland. The DFU is said to be financed by the Communist East. The NPD is generally considered to be the latest of the neo-Nazi parties. Neither the DP nor the GB-BHE presented candidates in 1965. The KPD (Communist Party of Germany) was dissolved in 1956. In 1961 all nonrepresented parties polled 5.7 percent of the vote together; in 1965 only 3.6 percent.

Stimmzettel

für die Bundestagswahl im Wahlkreis **63** Bonn am 19. September 1965

Sie haben 2 Stimmen

hier Erststimme	hier Zweitstimme
für die Wahl	für die Wahl
eines Wahlkreisabgeordneten	**einer Landesliste (Partei)**

	Erststimme			Zweitstimme	
1	**Dr. Adenauer, Konrad** Bundeskanzler a. D. Bad Honnef-Rhöndorf, Dr. Konrad-Adenauer- Straße 8 a	**CDU** Christlich Demokratische Union	◯	◯ **CDU**	**Christlich Demokratische Union** 1 Dr. Adenauer, Dr. Barzel, Dr. Schröder, Frau Brauksiepe, Katzer
2	**Nellen, Peter** Regierungsrat a. D. Düren, Tivolistraße 38	**SPD** Sozialdemokratische Partei Deutschlands	◯	◯ **SPD**	**Sozialdemokratische Partei Deutschlands** 2 Brandt, Dr. Heinemann, Dr. Arndt, Arendt, Figger
3	**Dr. Rahn, Rudolf** Geschäftsführer Düsseldorf, Pempelforter Str. 10	**FDP** Freie Demokratische Partei	◯	◯ **FDP**	**Freie Demokratische Partei** 3 Dr. Mende, Scheel, Zoglmann, Dr. Effertz, Frau Funcke
4	**Schwann, Hermann** Diplom-Landwirt Bergisch-Gladbach, Rommerscheider Str. 105	**AUD** Aktionsgemeinschaft Unabhängiger Deutscher	◯	◯ **AUD**	**Aktionsgemeinschaft Unabhängiger Deutscher** 4 Schwann, Hartung, Frau Dr. Fritz, Dr. Manstein, Knaup
5			◯	◯ **CVP**	**Christliche Volkspartei** 5 Vollmer, Schulte-Kellinghaus, Lühnen, Frau Mühlhoff, Thielkes
6	**Kampkötter, Günter** Inspektor der Berufsgenossenschaft Bonn, Hausdorffstr, 59	**DFU** Deutsche Friedens-Union	◯	◯ **DFU**	**Deutsche Friedens-Union** 6 Behrisch, Frau Dr. Kirchhof, Lukrawka, Graf von Westphalen, Sanb
7			◯	◯ **FSU**	**Freisoziale Union** 7 Schacht, Wandel, Kokaly, Triebler, Spiecker
8	**Dr. Schulze-Rauschenbach, Arno** Oberregierungsrat a. D. Bonn, Wasserland 2	**NPD** Nationaldemokratische Partei Deutschlands	◯	◯ **NPD**	**Nationaldemokratische Partei Deutschlands** 8 Prinz zu Salm, Schütz, Walendy, Dr. von Grünberg, Körner
9			◯	◯ **UAP**	**Unabhängige Arbeiter-Partei** 9 Kliese, Villmow, Plonz, Daumann, Drees

The Center Party had emerged out of the conflict between Catholics and Protestants, and even when that conflict had lost much of its meaning in the Weimar period, the Center had remained a Catholic party. But the suppression of both denominations by the Nazis forged mutual respect and a bond between them. Moreover, the brutal suppression of the most elementary human and ethical values which were committed under the swastika banner tended to underline the value of Christian ethics and morality. In fact, one of the most important of the resistance groups, the so-called Kreisau Circle, had a very pronounced Christian orientation, and the martyrdom of its leaders had its effect on the later creation of the CDU. It is not an accident that the men who met in Berlin in 1945 and founded the first group of the Christian Democratic Union were for the most part former inmates of Moabit prison and survivors of the abortive July 20, 1944, rebellion.

At about the same time another group met in Cologne, the traditional center of the Center Party, and came to similar conclusions, namely, that a purely Catholic party was now outdated and that Catholics and Protestants could and should unite. They founded the "Christian Democratic Party." Similar developments took place in other Laender. In December, 1945, representatives of these various groups met in Frankfurt, decided to adopt the unified term "Christian Democratic Union," and established a coordinating committee. Still a unified party was not established, and it was only after the need for cooperation had been demonstrated first in the Parliamentary Council and later in the first parliament of the Federal Republic that a unified national party was established at the party convention of Goslar in October, 1950. Only the Bavarian group, the Christian Social Union (CSU), insisted on remaining a separate entity. It joined the CDU parliamentary group, hence CDU/CSU, thus making it the largest in the *Bundestag*, and it agreed to far-reaching cooperation. But it continued to have its separate leadership and even within the parliamentary group maintained its own special organization as a *Land* group whose chairman is automatically Deputy Chairman of the CDU/CSU combined parliamentary group. In this the CSU followed the policy of its predecessor of the Weimar period, the Bavarian People's Party, which had also remained distinct and separate from the Center Party.

From the Center Party the CDU inherited an intramural quarrel over social policy. The Center Party had been a religious rather than a class party and hence combined socially and economically heterogeneous groups. In the CDU too, "left" and "right" groups were discernible. At first the left seemed to have the upper hand and both the "Cologne Principles" of 1945 and the "Ahlen Program" of 1947 contained a number of provisions strongly reminiscent of socialist demands. However, the "Duesseldorf Principles" of 1949 weakened these considerably, and after the currency reform, the principles of free enterprise championed by Professor Ludwig Erhard won out. To some extent this evolution must be credited to the strong personality of Dr. Konrad Adenauer who quickly emerged as the party's principal and undisputed leader. But it is also a fact that among the spectrum of parties which offered their services to the electorate, the CDU, although essentially a party of the center, constituted the right wing and therefore attracted the votes of all those who were opposed to socialism in every form. The weight of those voters was therefore also a factor in pushing the party to the right.

An additional factor of diminishing importance was that many of the leaders of the left wing were fugitives from East Germany, which did not inveigh against them in any way but which deprived them of their local clientele. As the economic policy of Erhard was crowned by unquestionable success, the economic and social course of the party was well set. This so-called "Social Market Policy" could be characterized essentially as free enterprise plus social safeguards. In reality, however, the government's program contained and still contains a great many control features, designed to hold prices, and especially wages, in line. Moreover, the government exercises great influence through large subsidies and through important publicly owned enterprises.

A crucial decision had to be made in 1949 when the first parliamentary government of the newly established German Federal Republic was organized. The elections of that year had given the CDU/CSU a small advantage over the Social Democrats, 31 percent over 29.2 percent. A coalition with either the Social

Democrats or the Free Democrats was available and Adenauer decided for the Free Democrats, partly because of his aversion to the SPD, especially its Chief, Dr. Kurt Schumacher; partly also out of fear that such a coalition would alienate the conservative element and drive it to the FDP without leading to a commensurate gain on the left where the place was already taken by the SPD.

From a partisan point of view, Adenauer's choice was justified by the events. From its slim plurality of 31 percent in 1949, the CDU/CSU rose to 45.2 percent in 1953 and to 50.2 percent in 1957. That the CDU/CSU declined from this high peak in 1961 to 45.4 percent was certainly not due to its initial decision. Nevertheless the CDU has retained a "left wing" which derives its origins from the former Christian Trade Union Movement but which, despite its size, has little influence. It was unlucky in that it lost through premature death several of its prominent leaders, especially the former Prime Minister of North Rhine-Westphalia, Karl Arnold.

The CDU was also successful in maintaining a balance in another delicate field, that of its denominational distribution. Although it started as a clearly interdenominational Christian party, at first the Catholic element prevailed among the leaders, the Protestant element among the followers. The historical tie to the Center Party and the fact that most of the Center's surviving leadership joined the CDU are responsible for this phenomenon. Even if the numerical balance had been different, the fact that the party's domineering figure, Konrad Adenauer, was a strict Catholic would have alone created the impression of Catholic dominance.

This situation might have become a real danger to the party's continued existence and unity, but Adenauer was well aware of this and moved with great care. His first designated successor, Hermann Ehlers, was a prominent Protestant. Although he died prematurely in 1954, Adenauer's gesture did not fail to impress the Protestants. Also many of Adenauer's important Cabinet ministers, especially Ludwig Erhard and the later Minister for Foreign Affairs, Dr. Gerhard Schroeder, were Protestants, as was the CDU President of the *Bundestag*, Dr. Eugen Gerstenmaier. Such conduct was also dictated by the reality of the party's backing in the country. The CDU remained very strong in predominantly Protestant parts of Germany, but only in the regions with Catholic majorities did the Protestant voters generally prefer other parties to it.

To sum up, it is fair to say that neither from its social policy nor from its denominational attitude is there likely to come major danger to the CDU's basic unity. That danger now lurks from another direction, the dispute over foreign policy, which will be discussed later.

The relationship between the Christian Democratic Union and the Christian Social Union is interesting and carries a number of unusual features. The CSU has managed to combine the advantages of a separate existence with those of belonging to a larger group. Its separateness gives it considerable leverage with the CDU party leadership and has resulted in a somewhat disproportionate number of CSU ministers in the cabinets of Chancellors Adenauer and Erhard. Its organic integration within the CDU/CSU gives its leaders full participation in the leadership of the combined group, and it is altogether possible that a CSU leader might well emerge as the chief figure of the combined group and as a future chancellor.

In predominantly Catholic Bavaria the Christian Social Union, being confined to that state, is of course largely Catholic. In the beginning, however, this did not mean a unified political line. Among the CSU's founders were the liberal Dr. Josef Mueller, who had worked with the anti-Nazi opposition, and the conservative Dr. Fritz Schaeffer. Later the strongly Catholic and archconservative Dr. Alois Hundhammer dominated the party, but this undoubtedly sincere man of great integrity was almost absurdly reactionary. In the field of education he introduced methods more at home in the 18th Century than in the 20th. From 1953 on, Hundhammer lost his hold on the party which became increasingly liberalized and interdenominational. But this development, which greatly strengthened the CSU's power in Bavaria, was also marked by the rise of one of the most gifted but also most erratic and controversial German politicians, the former Minister of Defense, Franz Josef Strauss. Strauss, who became General Secretary of the CSU in 1949 and its President in 1961, now dominates it completely.

The Christian Democratic Union, like the Federal Republic, cannot easily be imagined without the extraordinary, strong personality which shaped its rise from the ashes of defeat and destruction: Dr. Konrad Adenauer.

Adenauer is not only one of the most outstanding European statesmen of this or any period, but also its oldest. In this alone he constitutes a phenomenon which defies rational explanation. He was born in 1876 in Cologne, in that Rhineland which, while administratively a part of Prussia, was always distinct and separate from Prussia and even anti-Prussian. It was characterized not only by Catholic faith but also by an occidental orientation. From 1917 to 1933 Adenauer was Mayor of his native city, Cologne. From 1920 to 1932 he was also President of the Prussian State Council. Although a devout Catholic, he rebuked the conservative anti-republican Cardinal Faulhaber in 1922 for his attacks on the democratic foundations of the Weimar Republic, and with equal fervor and extraordinary personal courage refused on February 6, 1933, to dissolve the Prussian State Council in the face of the decrees issued in the name of President Hindenburg by the new Chancellor of the Reich, Adolf Hitler. In 1933 Adenauer was removed by the Nazis from all offices, and from then until the end of that regime he lived withdrawn in his home in Roehndorf tending his famous roses, except for a period of imprisonment in 1944–1945. Later on, at the zenith of his power, when asked when he would retire, he was fond of replying, "I have already had my retirement."

In 1945 he once again became Mayor of Cologne under military government, but ironically was dismissed by the British military governor for "incapacity." Later on Adenauer rarely missed an opportunity to remind British statesmen of that incident. 1946 saw him as the first chairman of the CDU in the British zone of occupation, and from that time on his leadership of that party remained assured.

His personality dominated the Parliamentary Council which drafted the new constitution, and it was almost a matter of course that he became the first Chancellor of the new German Federal Republic. In the world at large and often in Germany itself, the success of the four successive governments which Adenauer headed is often identified with the *Wirtschaftswunder* (Economic

Miracle) which marked Germany's amazing recovery from the destruction and the misery of war. The economic recovery of Germany, although not unique in Europe, is nevertheless astonishing. With a gross national product of 413.4 billion Deutsche Mark, Germany is second only to the United States. Its total annual export (16,228 million dollars) is also second only to the United States, while its total import (14,709 million dollars) place it third after the United States and Great Britain. (All figures are of 1964 United States Embassy compilation.) In gold holdings, in cement production, in automobile production, Germany is second to the United States. In steel and coal it ranks third after the United States (which is first in both cases), Japan and Great Britain respectively. In power production it ranks fourth (after the United States, Great Britain, and Japan) but second in the production of electrical equipment. Germany ranks second also in chemical products and machinery. The list could be continued indefinitely.

Certainly as head of the government during the formative years, Adenauer does deserve credit for this, especially as his extraordinary political instinct caused him to make the right decisions in the face of much adverse domestic and international criticism. But, as a matter of fact, Adenauer, like many strong political figures of history and of our times, was never very interested in economic problems and tended to leave them to his long-time Minister of Economics and later successor, Professor Ludwig Erhard. In this he was aided by a basically conservative political philosophy which made him sympathetic to Erhard's principles of free enterprise. Adenauer's enduring place in history is probably far more due to his decisions in the field of foreign policy than to any other factor or group of factors.

When the new Republic was established, it faced two principal problems in the world, beyond the obvious and imminent need for reconstruction: that of Germany's division and hence its quest for reunification, and that of Germany's relations to the former victors, particularly those in the West. Both problems were correctly identified as such both by Adenauer and by his great adversary, Dr. Kurt Schumacher, the first leader of the Social Democratic opposition party. But the emphasis which these two men placed on these issues differed, and therein lay their principal division. Schumacher felt that reunification had to come first and that Germany therefore should not tie herself too closely to the West. Adenauer, on the other hand, felt that reunification was rather remote and that it would be a long time before the Russians would be even willing to talk about it. To him, the principal requirement was Germany's firm incorporation into the Western world.

This seemed vital to Adenauer for a number of reasons: for one, having lived through much German history and especially its most recent and darkest part, Adenauer was skeptical about the newfound democratic spirit of his fellow countryman and he wanted them firmly tied to the more experienced Western democracies. For many years he seemed preoccupied with this, and often remarked in private conversations, "What will happen when I am no longer here?" For another reason, he was convinced that any agreement with the Soviet Union over the reunification of Germany was possible only if the West remained strong and united and if Germany played its full part. Together with two other great statesmen, Winston Churchill and French Foreign Minister Robert Schuman, he was convinced that the cornerstone of any such Western unity must be Franco-German reconciliation. To achieve this, he was willing to make almost any concession and even to court unpopularity as he did over the Saarland question. Like all great historical figures, Adenauer had his eyes firmly fixed on broad objectives from which he was not deterred by the exigencies of the moment. Few would deny that this constancy in his pro-Western attitude and the firmness of his objectives are largely responsible for the extraordinary speed with which defeated and despised Germany regained the respect of the world and her place among nations.

With his qualities of long range objectives, Adenauer combined a constancy in his direction, an imperturbable calm, and a highly accurate sense of timing, the secret weapon of all successful politicians. Thus Adenauer easily dominated not only the government but also his party. The late first President of the German Federal Republic, Theodor Heuss, once characterized Adenauer as *"ein Herr,"* a term which is difficult to translate; it connotes a masterful personality with the habit of command. At the same time Adenauer managed to be extremely popular. Although he is not a great orator he managed to speak very directly and personally to his audience, especially when he had its physical presence. Innumerable are the anecdotes and stories illustrating how Adenauer ran affairs without any serious interference from anyone. In that period, Adenauer and Germany were virtually identified with one another.

In the presence of such a strong personality, other outstanding leaders could not easily emerge in the Christian Democratic Union. Professor Ludwig Erhard became very popular and a vote-getter of first-rate proportions because of the success of his economic policies. But he was not a party leader in the same sense as Adenauer and his first steps in public life after World War II were as an expert rather than as a politician. In the field of foreign affairs, Adenauer insisted on remaining his own Foreign Minister until 1955 assisted only by a Secretary of State, Professor Walter Hallstein, later President of the Commission of the European Economic Community (Common Market). Even after Dr. Heinrich von Brentano became Foreign Minister in 1955, Adenauer remained solidly in charge of foreign policy.

In that period it was difficult to see other CDU leaders besides Konrad Adenauer. One of the most respected personalities was without doubt Dr. von Brentano who gained much credit for holding the party together in difficult days both before 1955 and after 1961 when he was Chairman of the CDU parliamentary group. His noble and self-effacing personality gained particular respect when he resigned as Foreign Minister in 1961 and when, in effect, he assured more than anyone else the transition from Adenauer to Erhard's chancellorship. A serious illness and death brought his career to an untimely end in 1964. His absence was sorely felt when great internal difficulties beset the CDU/CSU later.

Although a man of Adenauer's imperious temperament was bound to and did indeed come in for many bitter attacks, his position was not seriously questioned until 1959. By that time Adenauer was 83 years old and his succession had become a lively topic of conversation which, naturally, "the Old Man" (*der Alte*) as he was frequently called, did not encourage. Second in popularity to Adenauer was Economics Minister Ludwig Erhard, and in the country at large he was increasingly regarded as

Adenauer's logical successor. Adenauer himself, however, cordially distrusted Erhard and lost no opportunity to express his feelings, as is stated elsewhere in this book.

The crisis came to a head in 1959 because President Heuss's second and last presidential term was due to expire that year, and a successor had to be found. The Social Democrats announced their intention to support the candidacy of their Deputy Chairman, Professor Carlo Schmid, a brilliant orator and popular figure. The Christian Democrats found themselves without a suitable candidate. For a while Adenauer had pushed the candidacy of an intimate friend and collaborator, Dr. Heinrich Krone, Minister without portfolio, a respected conciliator within the CDU but relatively unknown in the country at large. In view of Schmid's popularity and greater public stature, there was danger that Krone's candidacy might not win out, and Adenauer withdrew his support.

Now Adenauer attempted to kill two birds with one stone. He urged the candidacy of Erhard for the presidency thereby hoping not only to eliminate Erhard from succession to the chancellorship and to shunt him off into the relatively powerless and ceremonial office of the presidency, but also to confront Schmid with a popular opponent. Erhard, however, understood this maneuver only too well and resisted. When Erhard proved adamant, Adenauer, who, by these maneuvers had placed himself in a difficult position, and who was encountering mounting criticism, found himself under pressure to become President himself.

For a while he accepted, but it became gradually clear that he posed conditions which could not be met. First he undertook a deep study of the Constitution and emerged with the statement that the office of the President was possibly much more important than people had thought. This declaration had a chilling effect on many political leaders and the press because it appeared that "Adenauer remains Adenauer" and that he hoped to dominate the political scene from the presidency as he had dominated it from the chancellorship. Whether his visit to France and the fact that he returned obviously impressed by General de Gaulle had something to do with this conception of the presidency is not known. At any rate, it was strongly rejected not only by the opposition but by the Christian Democrats themselves.

Secondly, Adenauer was clearly determined to name his own successor and to prevent the rise of Erhard. Whether he really wanted the then Finance Minister Franz Etzel to succeed him or whether he merely used Etzel for tactical reasons to weaken the Erhard forces is difficult to say. Rumors were numerous pushing the one or the other name forward in addition to that of Etzel. This maneuver too misfired and it became clear that if Adenauer were to become president, Erhard would in all probability succeed him. This realization caused "the Old Man" suddenly to reverse himself and to announce that he would lead the CDU into the 1961 elections after all, and that he expected to remain Chancellor. Instead of himself, he proposed a new candidate for the presidency, Dr. Heinrich Luebke, at that time Minister of Agriculture.

An outcry met this very blatant maneuver and for the first time it seemed as if Adenauer had lost some of his sure grip on his party and the ship of state. But again he had correctly judged the psychology of his party leaders and of parliament as a whole; the storm died down, Luebke was elected President, and the CDU/CSU again won the 1961 election with a combined total of 45.4 percent of the popular vote. To be sure, this was a decline from the 50.2 percent of the vote obtained in 1957 but it was still a very respectable showing.

Nevertheless the events of 1959 had opened the fissures of crisis within the party which would not heal again.[2] The crisis had begun over the succession to the presidency but had turned into a much longer dispute over the succession to the chancellorship. Erhard, the principal candidate, remained well out in front. But Adenauer's dislike for him, bordering on contempt, was a heavy handicap. Younger, ambitious leaders also felt that their time had come. Foremost among them were the then Minister of the Interior, the later Foreign Minister, Dr. Gerhard Schroe-

[2] The succession crisis is described by Gerhard Braunthal in *Cases in Comparative Government*, Boston, 1965, pp. 207–240. See also the broader study by Arnold J. Heidenheimer, *Adenauer and the CDU*, The Hague, 1960.

der, and the fast rising young Minister of Defense, Franz Josef Strauss.

Nor was the crisis only an internal one. Chancellor Adenauer had made the closest possible relations with America one of the principal aims of his government's policy. His relations to America, which were already excellent under the Truman-Acheson administration, became particularly intimate when General Dwight D. Eisenhower became President, and Adenauer established ties of deep personal friendship to Secretary of State John Foster Dulles. There was a great affinity of views and attitudes between those two statesmen who shared not only militant opposition to Communism, but also a deep religious faith. There is no doubt that Dulles's death constituted a profound personal blow to Adenauer that further deepened when the administration of President John F. Kennedy began in Washington.[3] There were no longer the old intimate ties, and perhaps the visual impression caused by the contrast between the young American President and the then 85-year-old German Chancellor was grist to the mills of those who felt that Adenauer had remained in power too long and that his policies had become too rigid. There is little doubt also that Adenauer suspected President Kennedy of being too optimistic about the probable evolution of East-West relations, while Adenauer's critics saw in the same events evidence that Adenauer had permitted his rigidity to lead Germany into isolation from the main currents of world affairs.

Another event also characterized the year 1961. It was in August of that year that the wall, which Germans came to call "the wall of shame," was erected by the Communist regime in East Germany to separate East and West Berlin. This sudden and nearly complete cut off caught the German government and its Western allies by surprise, and Adenauer's reaction was no more imminent and forceful than were those of the heads of other Western governments. This added to the widespread rumor that he had "lost his touch."

After the election of September, 1961, the new government proved extraordinarily difficult to form. The Free Democratic Party (FDP), which had been in steady decline and had polled

---

[3] Although Dulles was no longer Secretary of State when he died, Adenauer came to Washington for the funeral.

only 7.7 percent of the vote in 1957, had increased its forces to an unprecedented high of 12.8 percent. Clearly this was not a result of a greater popularity for the FDP, but rather illustrated a flight from the CDU of persons who were opposed to Adenauer's leadership but could not quite get themselves to vote for the opposition SPD. Encouraged by this temporary success, the FDP insisted on an unprecedented "coalition agreement" in which Chancellor Adenauer was forced to promise his resignation during the current term of the *Bundestag*. The FDP also demanded the "head" of Foreign Minister Heinrich von Brentano if for no other reason than that this was the best way in which they could get back at Adenauer.

The wrangle over the formation of the government proved so distasteful that the dignified von Brentano resigned from the Cabinet and resumed his office of Chairman of the CDU's parliamentary group. With this gesture he greatly increased his prestige, and played a vital role in overcoming the crisis which had now beset the CDU.

The fourth Adenauer Cabinet of 1961 had to sail on stormy waters. It witnessed several "affairs" of which the most dramatic was the "Spiegel affair." *Der Spiegel* is a sensational but often very well-informed mass-circulation weekly whose opposition to Chancellor Adenauer and to his Minister of Defense, Strauss, knew no limits. In 1962 an article on alleged shortcomings in the military establishment in Germany led to *Der Spiegel*'s prosecution for treason and induced Defense Minister Strauss to use the German military attaché in Madrid to pick up and bring home one of *Der Spiegel*'s vacationing editors. After Strauss had first denied and later admitted the affair, he was forced to resign, but Adenauer himself did not remain untouched by the consequences of these events.

More important, however, was the growing insistence by the Free Democratic Party and also by many CDU leaders that Adenauer should make good his bargain and resign. The crisis was bitter and prolonged because Adenauer was not only hesitant to leave power but was in particular trying desperately to prevent Erhard from succeeding him. However, the maneuvers which had proven so successful in the past proved unavailing this time, perhaps because even those CDU leaders who shared

Adenauer's poor opinion of Erhard felt that the Party absolutely needed Erhard's electoral appeal in the elections of 1965 if it was to prevail.

It was finally the skillful management of Dr. von Brentano which brought the crisis at least nominally to a close. Adenauer, finding that he could not delay his resignation any longer, left the chancellorship to Ludwig Erhard. However, he retained the Chairmanship of the CDU party whose actual day-by-day managerial functions were to be carried out by the party's "Executive Chairman," Hermann Dufhues. Otherwise the Cabinet remained virtually unchanged. In particular Gerhard Schroeder, who had become Foreign Minister after the resignation of Brentano in 1961, remained as Foreign Minister.

One might have believed that with this act the crisis within the CDU was over, but in reality it had only begun. One of the last significant official acts of Chancellor Adenauer was the signature of the Franco-German Friendship Treaty of January 22, 1963. Normally such an event would have been applauded by all and would have seemed like the fitting culmination of a career much of which was dedicated to friendlier relations between the two countries which had been hereditary enemies for hundreds of years. But times were far from normal. General de Gaulle had already begun his campaign to rid Europe of "Anglo-Saxon interference." Only a few days before this treaty was signed, on January 14, 1963, he had exploded a bomshell rejecting Great Britain's admission to the Common Market, thereby placing himself in sharp opposition to the policy of the United States. Under those circumstances, the Franco-German Friendship Treaty might have been interpreted as a demonstration in support of De Gaulle and in opposition to the United States, although this was certainly not intended. Moreover, many critics held that the establishment of elaborate consultation arrangements on a bilateral basis between France and Germany was in conflict with the spirit of the multilateral relationships established in the European Coal and Steel Community (Schuman Plan) and in the European Economic Community (Common Market). The fact that the German *Bundestag* adopted a preamble to the treaty which considerably softened its bilateral flavor merely underscored the existence of a sharp conflict.

It was clear that the new Chancellor, Ludwig Erhard, and his Foreign Minister, Gerhard Schroeder, did not wish to pursue a special relationship with France, that they favored a broader Atlantic alliance with the United States and a continuation of effort towards bringing Great Britain into Europe. As a consequence Franco-German relations began to deteriorate to the extent that General de Gaulle's campaign against the United States increased in intensity. It was on this issue that a new cleavage appeared.

The foreign policy of Chancellor Erhard and Foreign Minister Schroeder had the general support of the Social Democratic opposition but it ran almost immediately into a new opposition within the CDU/CSU itself. The leader thereof was the former Minister of Defense Franz Josef Strauss, but behind the scenes, and even sometimes in front of them, the Old Master, ex-Chancellor Adenauer, threw his considerable prestige into the scales against Erhard.

When Strauss had resigned from the government under the shadow of the *Der Spiegel* affair, most political observers believed that his political career had either ended or was seriously blighted for many years to come. This proved to be highly premature. Franz Josef Strauss is a man of outstanding talent marred by almost ungovernable temperament. He was born in Munich in 1915 and prepared for a secondary teaching career when the war broke out and he was drafted. After the war, since he had never been a Nazi, he was immediately appointed the Chief Officer of a county (*Landrat*) by American Military Government, and thereon rose rapidly as Germany became an independent nation again. As mentioned earlier, he helped to found the CSU in 1945, and became its General Secretary in 1949. In 1953 he became a Minister without portfolio in the second Adenauer Cabinet. In 1955 he was placed in charge of scientific and nuclear problems, and in 1956 at the age of 41 he became Minister of Defense. The newly re-established German armed forces having had an inauspicious start under Theodor Blank, Strauss threw his enormous energy into the fray in order to build a first-rate military instrument. Few would deny that he was on the whole not only very successful in this but also that he established firm civilian leadership and control over the new German army—a feature which was particularly important in view of Germany's past. At the same time he proved an excellent campaigner and an effective debater.

He took only a short vacation in 1962, after his ouster from office, before marching down the comeback trail. Curiously enough he started this via Israel to whose army he had rendered considerable assistance when he was Minister of Defense, thus creating something of a novelty for a major German political figure. He threw himself with great vigor into a *Land* election in Bavaria, and re-established his prestige in the victory he won. Finally he was overwhelmingly re-elected President of the CSU, which automatically made him Deputy Chairman of the CDU/CSU parliamentary group in the federal parliament. His firm hold over more than one-fifth of the CDU/CSU parliamentary group adds greatly to his political strength.

It was not long before Strauss attacked the government openly for neglecting its relationship to France. But it is also true that he and the other leaders of the intra-party opposition have always advocated the closest relations to the United States, especially in the field of defense. In this he never wavered, but he nevertheless asserted now that the government was neglecting its duty towards a more "European" policy and expressed sympathy for many of De Gaulle's views.

In this attitude Strauss was not alone. Criticism of Erhard and Schroeder had been mounting. Heinrich Krone and other leaders of the CDU supported Strauss. While the new Chairman of the CDU parliamentary group, Dr. Rainer Barzel, is nominally impartial, this young (born 1924) and gifted rising star of the CDU seemed at times to side more with Strauss than with Erhard and Schroeder. But perhaps the most powerful support of the Strauss group came from the old ex-Chancellor himself who, at 89, seemed to be of undiminished vigor and whose great skill and experience, when thrown into the balance, constituted a constant danger to the new Chancellor.

The Social Democratic Party

Although the Social Democratic Party (SPD) had been ruthlessly suppressed by the Nazis and its leaders killed or imprisoned whenever they did not manage to escape, the memory of the Party, its discipline and its achievement, were kept alive among the rank and file. Consequently it was not long after the end of the Nazi regime that the surviving leaders took up contact with one another. That was all the easier as many of them were immediately appointed by military government to various positions, combining as they did a solid anti-Nazi record with administrative experience. However, most of the top leadership of the Weimar Republic was gone and the new men who emerged were less well known nationally.

Among the Social Democrats who managed to keep in contact with each other during the Nazi regime, Wilhelm Leuschner, former trade union president and former Hessian Minister of the Interior, was by far the leading personality. In the government which the conspirators of 1944 had hoped to establish, he was to be Vice-Chancellor. The central theme of Leuschner's thinking had been the unity of the working people. Even on the day before his execution (September 29, 1944) he wrote, "Remain united! Rebuild," and as he was led to the gallows, his lips formed the word *"Einheit"* (unity).

It was largely due to the memory of this strong personality that many Social Democrats dreamed of establishing a unified Socialist Party based on the trade unions. Even after the true intentions of the Communists became clear and their pressure increased in Eastern Germany and Berlin, there was confusion among the Social Democratic leadership. The situation became clarified only after Dr. Kurt Schumacher rose to leadership in West Germany and embarked on an uncompromising struggle against the attempt of Communist infiltration and take-over. At a Party conference at Wenningen, on October 5, 1945, the lines of Schumacher's policy became clear. He rejected the concept of collective guilt against all Germans, he condemned all plans designed to turn Germany into a primarily agricultural country. With these actions, he established himself as the undisputed leader of the SPD and prevented a fusion with the Communists in West Germany.

Nevertheless, the Party was hard hit by the partition of Germany for it had been particularly in the eastern sections of the country that the SPD had been strongest. In 1946, 48.6 percent of the population of Berlin voted for the SPD, and before 1933,

34 percent of the population east of the Elbe River had voted for the SPD. Also Schumacher and Ollenhauer came originally from eastern Germany.

Schumacher's firm opposition to Communism gave him a certain freedom of action in the leadership of his Party. From the beginning he was determined to avoid the pitfalls of the Weimar Republic when the Social Democrats had been accused, albeit wrongly, of neglecting Germany's national interest. He opposed Germany's close integration in the West and on the whole conducted a policy tending to emphasize strongly his and his Party's independence. In particular the SPD and Schumacher stood up to the occupation powers whenever the occasion in their opinion required it. They vigorously opposed the dismantling of factories by the Allies and emphasized the necessity for German reunification. In domestic affairs they underlined the need for planning and the socialization of raw material-producing industry as well as government control over the financial structure of the country.

Traditionally the SPD is a strongly centralized Party with a considerable bureaucracy. It is by far the largest Party in terms of members in Germany who are quite thoroughly controlled by the national executive committee (*Parteivorstand*). Despite the Party discipline and despite its hold on the overwhelming majority of the German workers, the Schumacher policy of intransigent opposition to Adenauer's domestic and foreign policy did not pay off. On the contrary, while the CDU/CSU rose between 1949 and 1953 from 31 percent to 45.2 percent, the SPD declined slightly from 29.2 percent to 28.8 percent, which meant that it did not even pick up the 3.5 percent which the Communists lost in the same period.

Schumacher's policies might have met more determined opposition within the Party earlier had it not been for the extraordinary strength of his personality. He had lost an arm in World War I; he had spent over ten years in the most notorious concentration camps of the Nazi regime and as a result thereof had also lost a leg. Towards the end of his life, it almost seemed as if he had no body left but existed only as personified spirit. His piercing eyes, his commanding personality dominated all. Even those who disagreed with him within the Party found it almost impossible to oppose him outright. He did indeed protect his party from being accused of neglecting German national interests, but this was not enough to insure victory.

Schumacher died in 1952 and was succeeded by Erich Ollenhauer. For a while the negative policy of Schumacher continued, but obviously with very little result. Although the SPD governed ably in several of the Laender and in a large number of cities, the widespread suspicion against the "Red" party persisted among the middle classes. In particular, however, its national slogans demanding greater efforts towards reunification and lesser ties with the West proved unavailing. To be sure, not all Germans were certain that Adenauer's policy of meeting the Russians with strength and through Western unity was the best for Germany. To many, the SPD's argument that this was no way in which to negotiate Germany's reunification with the Soviet Union, may have had a ring of truth. But the weakness of the SPD argument lay in the implied assertion that the Soviet Union might be willing to concede reunification to any kind of Germany which it did not dominate. Hence, despite growing criticism of Adenauer's policy, the Social Democratic counter-argument fell on deaf ears. Added to this came the fact that the election campaign of 1957 was conducted by the Social Democrats under clearly demagogic slogans, especially the one which proclaimed "against atomic death," thereby implying that Adenauer and the CDU were somehow conducting a policy of German nuclear rearmament, which was both untrue and impossible. Although the SPD's voting strength increased slightly from 28.8 percent to 31.8 percent by 1957, largely as a result of the disappearance of smaller parties, the CDU/CSU reaped its greatest triumph by gaining an absolute majority with 50.2 percent of the vote. The general line of the SPD had clearly failed.

Defeat was all the greater as the Party had gone into the election with real hope because it had won a number of local and regional elections and hoped for better fortunes at the national elections. Now these gains were wiped out and in fact the whole election was a lopsided affair. The Adenauer government, already in power for eight years, should normally have been on the defensive while the opposition would have been expected to take the offensive. But with great shrewdness Adenauer had turned the tables and attacked the opposition with unremitted vigor.

It is to the considerable credit of the Social Democratic Party that it recognized these lessons and with resolution and courage undertook to remake itself. At the party congress of Bad Godesberg in 1959, the party made an about face. The last vestiges of Socialism were eliminated from the program, and free enterprise was endorsed, modified only by the demands of social justice. The nationalization of industries, never too popular among the German Social Democrats, was justified only as a counterweight to overly powerful concentrations of enterprises, and the whole subject was treated rather lightly. In contrast to its previous attitude, the Party now endorsed national defense and furthermore stated that "Democratic Socialism is rooted in Christian ethics." Moreover, the Party, which had voted against the Council of Europe and the European Coal and Steel Community, now endorsed European unification. History knows few examples of such a radical reorientation of a program.

There remained the weakness of the party's leadership. It was difficult even for the most dedicated Social Democrats to see the amiable and honorable but highly ineffectual Erich Ollenhauer as a true alternative to Konrad Adenauer. This was another feature which the Party now was determined to change. Although Ollenhauer remained technically as Party Chairman, the man who was proclaimed the Party's candidate for the Chancellorship was Berlin's mayor, Willy Brandt. His good looks, his dynamic personality, and the aura of a fighting mayor of Berlin were judged to be a better counterpoise to Adenauer than Ollenhauer's well-meaning but bumbling personality. Brandt's selection was also symbolic because he belonged to a group of Social Democratic mayors (the others being Max Brauer of Hamburg and Wilhelm Kaisen of Bremen) who had been highly critical of the SPD leadership. His background, however, proved a political handicap to him. He had fled to Norway in 1933 to escape Nazi persecution, and he became a Norwegian citizen. His opponents have alleged that he fought against Germany in Norwegian uniform, but this is false. The American press, in particular, tended to sympathize with Brandt, and portray him as a more formidable candidate than, in fact, he was.

However, the selection of Willy Brandt as the Party's standard bearer did not mean a transfer of the full power of Party leadership upon his shoulders. The man who had conceived the radical changes in the Party's attitude had been Fritz Erler. The man who had carried the changes through the Party Congress against all opposition had been Herbert Wehner. It was largely in the hands of those two men that the party fortunes now lay.

Herbert Wehner is probably the strongest personality in the Social Democratic Party. Born in 1906, he became a Communist for a short time in 1919 but then turned against them. He fought the Nazis as long as it was possible and then escaped abroad. After World War II he devoted himself to the reestablishment of the SPD machinery, especially in Hamburg, where he remained solidly entrenched. A Deputy Chairman of the Party, he has the Party bureaucracy well in hand. Despite his dislike for the limelight, he has grown in the confidence even of his opponents.

The outstanding brain of the Party and probably its greatest statesman is Fritz Erler. Erler was born in 1913 and although his formal education did not go beyond the secondary stage, he acquired a tremendous amount of knowledge through reading; he speaks both English and French fluently. During the Nazi period he worked in the underground, was arrested and spent many years in prison. A moderate and thoughtful individual, he was the engineer of the changes affected by the 1959 Party Congress, and is the undisputed foreign affairs and defense expert of the Party. He enjoys universal respect among friend and foe alike, and his questioning of ministers is well known for his thorough knowledge of the subject matter. He is also well known and highly respected abroad. When Ollenhauer died in 1964, Erler succeeded him as Chairman of the Parliamentary Group. If it were not for his somewhat colorless public image, it probably would have been he who carried the party's banner. But that role was given to Willy Brandt despite the fact that he had neither the strength and intra-party power of Wehner nor the intellectual force of Erler. In fact, Brandt's personal standing in the country and in the Party declined somewhat even before the 1965 elections.

In addition to Brandt, Erler, and Wehner, the SPD has a number of other notable leaders, among whom the Deputy Chairman of the *Bundestag*, Professor Carlo Schmid, is particularly noteworthy because of his brilliant intellect and his forensic abilities. Speeches by Schmid are probably the most brilliant heard in the *Bundestag* and are treated as an event. However, the somewhat belated and casual way in which he joined the SPD as well as his well-known taste for good living and his sharp tongue have made him less popular among the Party bureaucracy.

Ever since 1959 the tactics of the SPD have concentrated on one point; to win the confidence of the middle classes and to cast off any residue of a more radical past. The Party leadership has therefore consistently rejected the more intransigent demands of some of its more radical members. It has drawn the lesson from past electoral defeats that unless it is able to attract the middle class vote it can not win. By the beginning of 1965 it seemed that this goal had come within reach. The Party's constructive and moderate attitude had been demonstrated both on the national and international levels and in numerous Laender and local administrations. Both its domestic and its foreign policy were moderate and statesmanlike. The Party's devotion to the Atlantic Alliance and to European integration was now unquestionable. Its Party Congress of Karlsruhe in early 1965 was characterized by confidence that victory was near. The government of Chancellor Erhard was in difficulties and the public opinion polls put the SPD ahead (although Brandt's personal popularity trailed Erhard's by a very large margin). For the first time in its postwar history the SPD felt that victory lay within its grasp and that, if a majority might be difficult to achieve, a plurality seemed likely. But, as we shall see, this was not to happen.

The Free Democratic Party

The Free Democratic Party (FDP) had a difficult beginning. Its forerunners under the Weimar Republic, the German People's Party once led by Gustav Stresemann, and the Democratic Party, had already lost a great deal of their strength by the time the Weimar Republic had come to an end. Hence there were few cadres available through which a new beginning could be made.

The FDP emerged first in the Soviet zone and in Berlin in 1945 under the name of Liberal Democratic Party, but its collaboration with the Soviet authorities quickly became so intimate that it could be considered only a faceless instrument of that regime. In West Germany it first emerged in Wuerttemberg and Baden where German liberalism had been a tradition. Its first chairman was Professor Theodor Heuss, later first President of the Federal Republic. By 1946, it had established itself clearly as the principal third party. By 1948 the various independent parties of the different Laender united and adopted the common name Free Democratic Party.

Although the establishment of the FDP on a national basis had been accomplished, it retained many of its regional divergencies. In south and especially southwest Germany, the FDP tends to be reasonably liberal, while in the center and north of the country its orientation is farther to the right. To complicate the picture further, the Party tends to be anticlerical despite the fact that several of its leaders are Catholics, and it has therefore attracted a certain number of anti-Adenauer voters who could not see their way clear to shift to the Social Democrats.

In general one can say that in questions concerning religious schools and their like the FDP stands closer to the SPD than to the CDU, while on economic problems it is closer to the CDU and frequently to the right of it. At times the FDP has made strongly nationalist statements, and it was perhaps because of this that for a while there was a certain infiltration of former Nazis who grouped themselves around the controversial personality of Friedrich Middelhauve. This gave the FDP much trouble and it was only shortly before the 1953 elections that the Party finally purged this group from its ranks.

The decline which the FDP suffered in 1953 caused it considerable dissatisfaction and dissension. The dissatisfaction with Adenauer's policy increased and the Party, although it remained in the government, retreated into a confused position of semi-opposition. Its "enfant terrible" Dr. Thomas Dehler, had made embarrassing speeches in opposition to government policy even when he was Minister of Justice. When, after the 1953 elections, Adenauer refused to take him back into the Cabinet, he became Chairman of the FDP and expressed an increasingly antagonistic policy towards the Chancellor and his Cabinet. Thus in the great debate about the statute of the Saar, the FDP, with the exception of Vice-Chancellor Bluecher, voted against the government. In retaliation, Adenauer proposed an electoral system which would have deprived the Free Democratic Party of many of its seats, but in this he was finally forced to retreat. Then the FDP counterattacked in the most populous *Land*, Rhineland-Westphalia, and in February, 1956, reversed the coalition government there by suddenly bringing down the government of Prime Minister Karl Arnold in which it had participated, and in turn entered a coalition with the Social Democrats. But this coalition did not last very long.

None of this, however, helped the Free Democratic Party. Its decline seemed to be steady. Dehler had already retired from the chairmanship of the party in 1956 when the municipal elections ended in its defeat. He was replaced by the old liberal leader in Wuerttemberg-Baden, Rheinhold Maier. In 1957 the party's vote sank to 7.7 percent of the total vote cast. This was a blow to the so-called "young Turks" led by Wolfgang Doering who, from his stronghold in Duesseldorf, had engineered the coup against the Arnold (CDU) government. In their endeavor for an independent policy Doering and two other FDP leaders, Walter Scheel and Erich Mende, had gone into the Soviet zone in order to meet the leaders of the Liberal Democratic Party in Weimar. This, however, did not meet with much approval in the Federal Republic and probably contributed to the reversals which the Party suffered in 1957. Only in Baden-Wuerttemberg, the stronghold of Rheinhold Maier, did the party advance from 12.7 percent to 14.4 percent of the vote. It was a clear repudiation of both Dehler and the Duesseldorf "young Turks."

In the period between 1957 and 1961 the Free Democratic Party attempted a difficult game. It tried at one and the same time to be to the right and to the left of the Christian Democratic Union; to the right in order to attract the unorganized conservatives, ex-Nazis and the like, to the left in the English and American sense of that word, in order to attract those who had become disappointed or had been rejected by the two larger parties.[4] It continued to base some of its propaganda on the peculiar argument that a two-party system towards which Ger-

---

[4] In German, and even more in French, the word "liberal" connotes free enterprise, no government interference with business, etc., in other words

many seemed to be going was somehow undemocratic and did not offer the voter a sufficient choice.

There is little doubt that the fortunes of the FDP would have continued to decline had it not been for the presidential succession crisis and the general crisis within the CDU which in the opinion of many voters put Adenauer in a bad light. Thus in the elections of 1961 the Liberal Party became a home for those who no longer wished to accept Adenauer but who could not quite get themselves to vote for the SPD opposition. As a result, the FDP obtained an all-time high of 12.8 percent. That and the decrease in the strength of the CDU made it possible for the FDP to exert important concessions before it would agree to enter another coalition government. In fact, it was the struggle over these conditions which made the 1961 government crisis so prolonged. Pivotal point of the FDP conditions was the demand that Adenauer should retire after a suitable period but not too long after the elections. After much difficulty, as we have seen in preceding pages, this condition was accepted and the FDP entered the fourth and last Adenauer Cabinet. However, as a symbol of its resistance to Adenauer, the Party's Chairman of the Parliamentary Group, Erich Mende, did not enter the Cabinet and let it be known that he would not do so until Adenauer had retired. (He became in fact Vice Chancellor in the first Cabinet of Ludwig Erhard.)

As the Free Democratic Party approached the 1965 elections, it again sought a separate course of action in order not to be identified with the Christian Democratic Union. It found this in emphasis on nationalism, a return actually to an earlier position which demanded that Germany's national interests be placed ahead of both European integration and the Atlantic Alliance, but without opposing either. This line met with only moderate success because equally or more authentic nationalists were to be found in the CDU/CSU. In the opinion of most observers, the 1961 elections constituted a fluke, and nothing would hold up the steady decline of the FDP and Germany's eventual joining of

---

that which in the United States would be called "conservative." In Germany the term liberal has, however, retained a second meaning which is somewhat closer to the Anglo-American one.

the ranks of two-party countries. This seemed indeed the case after the 1965 elections.

The Other, Smaller Parties

The Christian Democratic Union/Christian Social Union, the Social Democratic Party, and the Free Democratic Party are the only parties which have survived in the *Bundestag*. Compared to them, all other parties fade into insignificance. The German Party (DP) has maintained a certain strength in lower Saxony where it had its roots in the former Hanoverian movement. However, it never was an independent party in the true sense of the word. It always collaborated closely with the CDU and in fact was saved from disappearance in 1957 only by the help of the CDU. In 1961 the DP attempted to survive in coalition with another splinter party, the Refugee Party, called All German Federations —Federation of the Homeless and Disenfranchised (GD/BHE) which had already lost its representation in the *Bundestag* in 1957. But this maneuver did not succeed. Before this event, several outstanding DP leaders, especially Hans Joachim von Merkatz, had deserted it and joined the CDU. In the 1965 elections the GD/BHE did not even present any candidates.

It was natural that after the war there should be persistent efforts to marshal the remnants of the former Nazi voters and create some sort of more or less overt neo-Nazi movement. These efforts, however, were not crowned with success. In 1950 an openly neo-Nazi party called Socialist Reich Party *(Sozialistische Reichspartei)* appeared under the nominal leadership of the former Major Ernst Rehmer who had been instrumental in suppressing the July, 1944, uprising in Berlin. This SRP caused alarm when in 1951 it obtained 11 percent of the vote in a *Land* election (Lower Saxony). However, it did less well elsewhere and was rent by internal dissension. It was outlawed in 1952 by the Federal Constitutional Court.

A successor, the German Reich Party *(Deutsche Reichspartei)* obtained only 1.1 percent of the vote in 1953 and 1.0 percent in 1957. In 1965 yet another successor party was presented to the electorate, calling itself National Democratic Party of Germany

(*Nationaldemokratische Partei Deutschlands*—NPD) and polled 2.0 percent of the total vote.

On the extreme left, the Communist Party had polled 5.7 percent in 1949 and sent 15 deputies into the *Bundestag*. However, in 1953 it dropped to 2.2 percent and lost all its seats under the 5 percent-minimum vote clause of the electoral law. It was dissolved in 1956 by the Federal Constitutional Court. In 1965 a new party made its appearance, called German Peace Union (*Deutsche Friedensunion*—DFU) and composed of former Communists, ex-Socialists, and pacifists. It is widely believed that this group receives much of its financial support from the Communist East. In the 1965 elections it received 1.3 percent of the vote.

Other parties are too insignificant to mention. Some are purely regional like the Bavarian Party (BP) or the Christian People's Party (CVP) from the Saarland. Others, like the Action Group of Independent Germans (AUD) and the Free Social Union (FSU) have little appeal, obtaining 0.1 percent or, in the case of the FSU even less, in the 1965 elections.

The Political Parties After the 1965 Elections

The elections of September 19, 1965, had a profound and, in all probability, long-range significance. They were the first in which Chancellor Ludwig Erhard was truly in charge, the first national elections of the post-Adenauer era. True, the seemingly indestructible old ex-Chancellor was around, and proved himself the liveliest and also perhaps the most interesting of all the campaigners of any party. But this time the people felt called upon to decide for or against Ludwig Erhard, not for or against Konrad Adenauer, and they were quite aware of the fact that this was the essential question.

This was an election in which the German polling institutions did not cover themselves with glory. They had all, without exception, predicted a neck-to-neck race between the CDU/CSU and the SPD although they had agreed that an uncommonly large number of voters (at times as many as 25 percent) had declared themselves undecided. The subsequent results indicated that a good many of those "undecided" were merely expressing some irritation with the CDU and in some cases with the FDP which in the last analysis did not prove significant enough for them to shift their allegiances.

If the SPD made some gains, adding 3 percent to their total vote, they clearly did not take strength away from the CDU which also increased its percentage by very nearly the same figure: 2.3 percent. Although both principal parties had obviously made gains at the expense of the FDP and other third parties, there had been some curious shifts in their own midst. Both lost in most of their habitual strongholds, or, to be more precise, they gained fewer votes there than they obtained elsewhere. Hence the SPD won votes in excess of its national mean in such CDU (or CSU) strongholds as Bavaria, Rhineland-Palatinate, and the Saarland, but was disappointed in its own "fortresses" of Hesse, Lower Saxony, Bremen, and Hamburg. To be sure, this trend was not uniform; in the industrial Ruhr area of North-Rhine-Westphalia, where the Social Democrats are traditionally strong, they improved their position; contrariwise, in the normally strong CDU-voting *Land* of Baden-Württemberg, the CDU further improved its position.

However, the over-all effect of the "weakening of the bastions" was the suspicion that both major parties now had to contend with a larger floating vote and that they were possibly less secure. This might mean that if the CDU/CSU plurality, and especially Chancellor Erhard himself, were to disappoint the voters in the future there could be considerable shifts; but all that was speculation. The only provable fact was that despite seemingly excellent chances and after sixteen years of opposition, the SPD was no nearer to power than it had been before.

The outcome was a good deal more favorable than the CDU/CSU had expected, and a good deal less than the SPD had felt entitled to. For both parties these elections posed many problems and questions regarding their future course.

For the Christian Democratic Union the victory was not only highly gratifying but underscored without the slightest doubt the pivotal significance of Ludwig Erhard. He had in fact proven himself to be that *Wahllokomotive* (election engine) which his reputation had alleged. Although this was by no means a one-man victory, Erhard had clearly been "the engine which pulled the rest of the train." Yet it would be a mistake to say that it had been due to his dynamic personality or his oratorical gift of flair; this is not the figure which Ludwig Erhard cuts or attempts to cut. Attendance at his election rallies actually fell off considerably as election day approached, and his speeches were rather dull, pedantic, and repetitive. In fact, many of his listeners probably failed to understand what he was talking about, and he had neither the popular flavor nor the "give them hell" attitude of Adenauer. But none of these things seemed to matter. Ludwig Erhard, by his past performance and even perhaps by his rotund appearance with the eternal cigar clamped into his mouth, was the symbol of German recovery, of the "economic miracle," and it was quite clear that the majority of the German people preferred to keep things as they were. Even the opposition SPD seemed to have recognized this basic mood when it adopted the slogan *"Sicher ist sicher"* (literally "be careful," but it might be translated more idiomatically as "don't rock the boat"), an astonishing slogan for an opposition party.

The symbolic force of Erhard's personality and record were all the more enhanced as the election campaign stressed domestic issues. This did not mean that foreign policy issues were secondary—quite the contrary. On most domestic issues there was a large measure of identity between the views of the Erhard government and of the opposition. The real conflict was between Erhard and his foreign minister Gerhard Schroeder on the one hand, and ex-Chancellor Konrad Adenauer and former defense minister Franz Josef Strauss on the other.

The opposition found it difficult to profit from these intraparty quarrels within the CDU/CSU without supporting Erhard. The only course open to the Social Democratic Party was to underline the fact of disunity within the government party, and accuse Erhard of fumbling the ball. That was not enough to make a strong impression on the voters. "Opposition . . . is the art of sawing off the branch on which the government is sitting in such a way that you can sit on it yourself," said SPD Chief Erler in the 1961 campaign. It remained too delicate a task in 1965.

Erhard's victory did not resolve the foreign policy differences, which also reflected differences between personalities within the CDU/CSU. True, the Chancellor's position had become very much stronger now that he had been returned to office in his own right. But the CSU retained its independent position and its leader, Strauss, had reaffirmed his hold on it in the 1965 election, due to the notable progress it had made in Bavaria.

Nevertheless, the personal victory of Erhard made it less profitable for the intra-party opposition to attack him head-on. Hence, their target remained the Foreign Minister, Gerhard Schroeder, whose somewhat cold personality has not always made him friends when he needed them, and who did not have a powerful political position in his home constituency of Duesseldorf. Schroeder has proven himself an effective foreign minister with a steady hand on the helm, and a man of character capable of occasional feats of great brilliance despite an indifferent health, but he has remained in office only due to Chancellor Erhard's support. It is, therefore, conceivable that at one time or another the Chancellor might feel induced to strike a bargain with his opponents which might end in Schroeder's resignation. However, Erhard has been in politics too long not to realize that those who strike at Schroeder strike really at him, and that Schroeder's sacrifice would not cool the temper of the battle.

However, the bitter in-fighting within the CDU/CSU and the coalition in general, which preceded the formal election of Ludwig Erhard as Chancellor on October 20, 1965, revealed the serious dissension within. The "nationalist" opposition and its most outspoken leader, Franz Josef Strauss, gained a few points. True, Strauss had been unable to unseat his principal targets in the cabinet, Foreign Minister Schroeder and Vice-Chancellor Mende (FDP). It is in fact doubtful that Strauss really expected this. But he extracted from the highly reluctant FDP a formal "declaration of rehabilitation" (*Ehrenerklärung*) in which the FDP exonerated him for conduct which it had previously declared made Strauss morally ineligible for a cabinet post. This referred to Strauss' admission of his part in the *Spiegel* affair after having first denied it in Parliament. This favored Strauss' resignation from the Cabinet and produced the election of the FDP from which the above-mentioned declaration now faced Strauss.

One might assume that the Democratic Party's real views on

Strauss had probably not changed, but this declaration made it impossible for it to prevent his eventual return to the cabinet. Then came Erhard's formal offer of a cabinet post to Strauss, which the latter declined. After Strauss revealed this offer in a television interview on October 22, 1965, without meeting any contradiction from Erhard, it became clear that there could now be no future objection from Erhard either, unless new conflicts or "incidents" were to develop. Strauss was entitled to regard these moves as at least a partial victory for himself. Moreover, his various feuds within the Christian Social Union, with such personalities as the colorful Karl Theodor Freiherr zu Guttenberg, had also been settled amicably, and a close associate, Dr. Richard Jaeger, entered the cabinet as a fifth CSU Minister (Justice). Previously, the CSU had had four representatives in the cabinet.

If there was one loser in the infighting, it was former Chancellor Konrad Adenauer who, in the opinion of many observers, had carried his attacks against Schroeder too far and for too long. His influence in the CDU was now likely to diminish and, at the age of 90, he was now scheduled to lose the chairmanship of the CDU as well. But the old warrior's personal eclipse did not seemingly diminish his cause. The fight against Schroeder would clearly continue undiminished, supported by a vague feeling in political circles—unproven but widely shared—that a growing portion of the electorate favored a more "independent," German foreign policy, a policy which was not necessarily less "Western," but which would be less inclined allegedly to "subordinate" specifically "German" concerns to broader Western or "Atlantic objectives."

What heightens the intensity of the struggle is the fact that the attack on Schroeder is merely a phase in the struggle for Erhard's eventual succession. Hence it is likely to go on for quite some time, especially as at least one of the principal figures, Franz Josef Strauss, is determined to return to the cabinet and eventually to rise to the top. In the meantime, much of the party's ability to function as a unit depends upon the effective floor management of the party's forces in the *Bundestag.* The role of the party's majority leader in the House (*Fraktionsvorsitzender*—chairman of the parliamentary group), Dr. Reiner Barzel, is, therefore, one of pivotal importance exceeding that of many a cabinet minister. Many see in this exceedingly able and young (born 1924) man the future leader and Chancellor; all the more so as his ability for compromise has seen the party over many a rough spot. He is consequently accumulating fewer enemies than the front runners, and he is in no hurry. Inasmuch as such events can be forecast over longer periods of time in the topsy-turvy of party politics, Reiner Barzel looks like a good bet for the eventual winner.

If men like Barzel and the much older Heinrich Krone are able to keep the ambitious front runners from cutting each other to pieces, then the Christian Democratic Union is likely to enjoy a still longer term in office.

Ever since the re-establishment of the Social Democratic Party in Germany, it has steadily progressed, except for a slight dip in 1953. But this progress has not been sufficiently fast nor of the right kind to bring it much closer to success. In 1949, less than 2 percent separated the SPD from the CDU/CSU. In 1953 and 1957 the gap widened to 16.4 and 18.4 percent respectively, only to shrink to 9 percent in 1961, and to 8.3 percent in the most recent elections in 1965. But these changes are deceptive. Both the SPD and the CDU/CSU gained from the gradual disappearance of small parties, but now that reservoir of voters has nearly disappeared except for the FDP, and it is also diminishing. Hence the day is not far distant when either of the two principal parties will be able to make substantial progress only from each other. Seen in this light, a gap of 8 to 9 percent is rather a formidable one to overcome. Mathematically the gap would seem small because, when third parties are excluded or stable, a 2 percent gain would narrow the CDU/CSU–SPD gap by 4 percent. But thus far the SPD's ability to cut into the CDU/CSU vote has been offset by losses in SPD strongholds.

The SPD leadership was quite aware of this state of affairs. Both in 1961, and even more so in 1965, its principal thrust was toward respectability, an all-out attempt to convince middle-class voters that the Social Democratic Party had given up all plans of Socialist experimentation and nationalization, let alone revolutionary upturns. As one of the party's opponents put it somewhat caustically, the SPD was out to prove "that it was the best CDU of them all." In like manner this Socialist party which had once voted against the Schuman Plan and NATO had become the strongest defender of European integration and the Atlantic alliance. Nor could these changes be attributed to opportunism. Apart from the change in leadership from Schumacher to his successors, there was the understanding which grows with experience, and the realization that in modern industrial countries the great masses of the voters are located in the middle of the road and that the widespread belief that those voters are looking for sharp alternatives is a legend in Germany, as well as elsewhere.

This evolution had not come easily; it had been hard fought. It was, therefore, a matter of bitter disappointment that the elections of 1965 did not produce the expected progress. True, the party gained 3 percent over 1961, but the gap between the two parties had not substantially lessened. Moreover, in the face of disunity in the CDU ranks and of a number of government fumbles, a substantial number of voters had evidently hesitated (hence the misleading public opinion poll figures) and then returned to the CDU. The SPD had been successful in marshalling an impressive number of intellectuals in its behalf and seemed to have made some inroads among the youth. Yet, in the end, that did not make much difference.

It would be understandable if the SPD leaders were to ask themselves the depressing question as to what else they could have done to win, and whether they are likely to go to the polls again very soon under any more favorable circumstances. Barring major upheavals or an economic crisis of some proportion, they might well wonder whether they are condemned to the position of a loyal and respectable opposition, and this in stark contrast to the fact that in several of the Laender the SPD has governed effectively for a great many years and has earned the respect even of its opponents.

Under those circumstances, the Social Democrats cannot avoid internal pressures. Those in the ranks who have accepted the shift to moderation only grudgingly are bound to demand a turn to the left. They are not likely to be successful. But the battle will be on. Moreover, in a general atmosphere in which the younger generation is likely to ask for a more independent German policy, there will be a temptation to urge the SPD leadership to take a more "flexible" attitude towards the Soviet Union. Some may wish to become more than flexible since Germany's youth, while still strongly anti-communist, are perhaps more willing to experiment with East-West relations than have been their elders who remember the Stalin era only too well.

In view of the discipline of the SPD and the strong reasoning power of its present leadership, especially Herbert Wehner and Fritz Erler, the past standpoint is likely to prevail. But the struggle is equally likely to shake the party and to contribute to the present leadership's becoming used up. In that case, younger forces will come to the fore, among them Helmut Schmidt (born 1918) who has earned the respect of his colleagues and opponents, and who has risen fast in the party's councils, especially in matters affecting foreign policy and defense. A period of serious self-examination lies ahead for the SPD.

One thing that would help it greatly would be a "great coalition," that is, a coalition government composed of Social Democrats and Christian Democrats. Had the outcome of the election actually been as close as the polls indicated it would be, this might have been a possibility. For a variety of reasons, it was advocated or presented as a possible alternative within CDU circles. Former Chancellor Konrad Adenauer, while hitting the SPD hard in the campaign, was careful not to rule out such a possibility and even gave it some encouragement. And as politics makes strange bedfellows, Franz Josef Strauss blew the same horn. The SPD leaders themselves were careful not to let the passion of election opposition go too far lest the relations between the two principal parties were poisoned and cooperation become impossible. Entry into such a coalition would constitute the final proof of the SPD's respectability, and the excellent qualities of some of its leaders, especially Fritz Erler, would undoubtedly make an impressive contribution to the science of statecraft. But it is probably for the same reason that Chancellor Ludwig Erhard has rejected such a coalition and it is, therefore, unlikely to occur in the foreseeable future.

Many commentators described the Free Democratic Party as the principal loser of the 1965 elections. This is technically true but oversimplifies the situation. It is correct that the FDP declined from a height of 12.7 percent in 1961 to 9.5 percent in

1965. However, the 1961 results had always been considered a fluke and untypical of the long-term fortunes of the FDP. Prior to 1961, the FDP had been in a steady decline. From 11.9 percent in 1949 it went down to 9.5 and 7.7 percent in 1953 and 1957 respectively. Then when Adenauer engaged in the already-discussed maneuvers over the presidency in 1961 and then clung to the Chancellorship, his loss of prestige was such that an important number of CDU voters were alienated and sought an outlet for their protest without voting SPD. The FDP provided this outlet and thereby steeply rose to 12.7 percent. But few people assumed that there were permanent gains. It was taken for granted that most of this increment would revert to the CDU once the succession question had been settled. That the FDP was able to retain 9.5 percent of the vote rather than dropping to the 7.7 percent of 1957, or below, that constitutes a limited success and would indicate that, while the party's eventual decline has probably not been prevented, it has at least been slowed down.

In the long run, the FDP's chances have not become brighter. Under Ludwig Erhard's leadership the CDU's ranks seem to be wide enough to take in most non-SPD voters. The suspicion that the CDU was under excessive Catholic influence has since been very substantially modified by the fact that both Chancellor Ludwig Erhard and Foreign Minister Gerhard Schroeder are Protestants, as is the president of the *Bundestag*, Eugen Gerstenmaier. Erich Mende, the leader of the FDP, on the other hand, is a Catholic.

For a time the "third position" of the Free Democratic Party will continue to have a certain appeal. A number of voters seem to believe that a system with only two overwhelmingly strong parties is not desirable. A certain note of nationalism is also noticeable in FDP ranks, but this is unlikely to become an element of great appeal, because one of its strongholds, Baden-Wuerttemberg, has deep roots in the liberal rather than the national tradition of the party.

In the post-election coalition infighting of September-October, 1965, it seemed for a while that the Free Democrats were toying with the idea of becoming the party of "national(ist)" opposition. Two of its most energetic leaders, Knut von Kuehlmann-Stumm and Thomas Dehler, appeared to be taken with this idea. It almost certainly contributed to that party's unexpected firmness in that crisis. However, the FDP had taken too many contradictory positions to stay such a course, and the more moderate tendencies of Erich Mende prevailed.

It may still be assumed that Germany will continue its slow path towards a two-party system. However, that trend has slowed down, and the FDP can expect to hold on to a portion of the electorate for quite some time before it approaches the danger zone of the 5 percent rule below which point no party receives representation in the *Bundestag*. (See page 122.)

Interest and Pressure Groups

The political life of every country knows the phenomenon of interest and pressure groups. This is natural because citizens are not only voters who cast their ballots in the interest of the greater national good, they are also members of professions, clubs, and causes that wish to encourage and discourage any number of legislative or executive acts. The implementation of these interests, however, depends to a large extent on the political system of each country. In the United States, where Senators and Congressmen only rarely respond to any form of national party discipline and where they are dependent on their own local support, it is logical that interest groups make them at least part of their target area. In Germany, on the other hand, where party discipline is of a high order, such tactics would not often be profitable and interest and pressure groups are therefore organized primarily to work on the government or on the leadership of the political parties.

This does not mean that in Germany pressure groups are not represented in the halls of parliament. Quite the contrary. In fact the most important pressure groups "own" a number of parliamentary seats. In the Social Democratic Party this refers primarily to the powerful German Trade Union Federation which is officially nonpartisan but whose great majority of leaders and followers are Social Democrats. Among the CDU and the FDP there are a number of parliamentary seats which are in effect controlled by representatives of large industries. However, the function of these "inner pressure groups" is not to vote differently from the bulk of their party's deputies but rather to watch over the party's conduct in parliament and to influence it where possible. Today there are well over two hundred offices of various groups and interests in Bonn and the coming and going of their representatives could fill many pages.

One of the most active is the German Farmers' Federation (*Deutscher Bauernverband*) which represents its members with great militancy. One of the best known groups is the Federation of German Industry (*Bundesverband der deutschen Industrie*) whose chairman, Fritz Berg, is a well known public figure, and one of whose members is a leading banker, Hermann J. Abs. In contrast to other countries where the effectiveness of industrial pressure is modified by the conflicting interests existing within associations of industry, the German Federation is in a more powerful position because of the dominant interests of heavy industry, especially iron and steel.

Yet another category of pressure groups are the representatives of refugee organizations generally organized by the areas from which their members came, such as Sudetenland, Silesia, East Prussia, etc. These regional groupings (*Landmannschaften*) usually hold annual public meetings where nationalist talks have often attracted public attention. Less attention has been focussed on their more quiet legislative work which has been aided by the fact that a considerable percentage of the deputies of all parties are former refugees or expellees, although not all of them feel necessarily identified with those groups.

Still another type of pressure group are the veterans' organizations, but their effectiveness has suffered from divergent political orientation and especially from the neo-Nazi excesses of some of their imprudent leaders such as ex-parachutist, General Ramke. Moreover, it is in the nature of things that their members must die out and cannot be replaced.

An interest and pressure group of a somewhat different kind is the labor union movement. There are over 8 million organized workers in Germany—about two-fifths of the entire German labor force. Of those 8 million, the overwhelming majority, about 6.4 million, are organized in the powerful German Labor Federation (*Deutscher Gewerkschaftsbund—DGB*). When this organization was established in 1949, it was intended to have one all-encompassing labor organization and not to return to the political and religious splits of the labor union movement of the Weimar Republic. This came near to success without quite accomplishing it. Two groups, office workers and civil servants, formed their own organizations (*Deutsche Angestellten-Gewerkschaft*—DAG, and *Deutscher Beamtenbund*—DBB). In 1955, Catholic trade union groups, irritated over the DGB's overwhelming support of Social Democratic aims, left it and formed once again a German Christian Labor Union Movement (*Christliche Gewerkschaftsbewegung*—CGB). However, with little over 200,000 members, it has remained the smallest group outside the DGB.

Under its first chairman, Hans Boeckler, the nonpartisan character of the German Labor Federation was fairly well maintained although many labor leaders considered this a handicap. From 1953 on, however, the DGB became more openly partisan in favor of the Social Democratic Party, as stated above, which led to the departure of the Christian Labor Union Movement. The power of the DGB to influence political decisions has been somewhat mitigated by the long period during which it imposed self-discipline upon itself to refrain from strikes in order not to hurt Germany's reconstruction. A major credit for the "economic miracle" therefore belongs to the German labor movement. On the other hand, the bitter struggle over "co-determination" (membership of labor representatives on boards of management) on which both the unions and the Social Democrats were very keen in the 1950s, proved to be a disappointment in that it turned out to constitute neither a major threat to industrial management nor a major gain to labor union power. Labor's representatives, seeing the whole picture of an industry, often acquired an industry viewpoint very much to the surprise and disgust of their followers. The fact that a high percentage of the *Bundestag*'s members are at least nominally union members is not very meaningful because many deputies, especially among the SPD, pride themselves on their workers' origin, and demonstrate this by remaining labor union members. In actual practice they are frequently guided by other considerations, and moreover there is the ever present factor of party discipline.

Although interest and pressure groups have played an impor-

tant role in German politics for a long time, their study is relatively recent, largely under the influence of American political
science and sociology. The German public often reacts unfavorably to their activities. Since by the nature of things pressure groups frequently act in the shadows, the manner in which
they have been known to influence decisions, and even appointments and promotions within ministries, has come in for a good
deal of criticism. Dealing with them has also become a first-rate
political factor. Former Chancellor Adenauer frequently took it
upon himself to deal with pressure groups, especially professional
and business associations, rather than leaving them to his respective ministers. This tended to enhance both his power and that
of the interest groups.

As in most countries, pressure groups work in a great variety
of ways in Germany. There is a massive "educational" effort
directed at ministries, party leaders, and deputies. There are the
press campaigns, in which especially the Farmers' Federation and
the refugee organizations excel, although often the seemingly
excessiveness of their demands has proven counterproductive over
time. Sometimes these organizations concentrate their fire on a
specific person, sometimes a minister, but their ratio of success
has not been too high.

The labor unions have steadily grown in power and organiza-
tional skill. They maintain training schools for their cadres and
have accumulated huge strike funds. However, on the whole,
their attitude has been moderate and they have been known to
make common cause with the employers when a common threat
appears on the horizon. But also the fact that strikes are distinctly
unpopular in Germany has influenced their stand.

German Reunification as a Political Issue

Modern Germany, despite its post-war rejuvenation and bright
future, has a painful and seemingly permanent grievance: it is a
divided country. By permanent, I do not necessarily mean to see
into, and forecast, the future. But a divided Germany is already
of long duration, and the end is by no means in sight. This
grievance permeates political life at many different levels and

takes many forms. All public opinion polls and analyses show that the impact of the division of Germany on German political life is steadily growing. No political party, no politician, can afford to ignore it. In the formulation of Germany's foreign policy it is ever present. Yet in spite of its magnitude, this problem is not easy for Germans or foreigners to grasp.

The problem of a divided country is quite substantially different from that of a country which has lost a part of its territory to an alien power. Such "lost provinces" may indeed affect a nation deeply; history abounds with examples. But the loss to a foreign country of even the most cherished provinces, usually as the result of losing a war, does not affect the national fabric or identity of that which is left. Between the Franco-Prussian War and the end of World War I, France had lost Alsace-Lorraine. This loss was keenly felt in France, it was an object of almost national mourning and its everpresence was epitomized in the slogan, "Let us always think of it, but let us never speak of it" which, while not obeyed—since there has been plenty of speech —illustrates the depth of national feeling. But at no time was the identity of France in question. On the contrary, the keen sense of a common loss made the nation even more aware of its own identity.

It is quite different when a country is divided. The line which divides East and West Germany, or more officially the German Federal Republic and the German Democratic Republic, is totally artificial, the result of politics, power, and a war lost. It separates not two countries of different history, language, and culture, but two parts of one country with identical history, language, and culture. While this dividing line lasts, it imprints the stamp of the impermanent, the provisional, and the undesirable on both Germanies.

National awareness and identity are two of the mainsprings of human endeavor and progress, but it is difficult for modern Germans to identify themselves with such entities as the Federal Republic or the DDR. This difficulty exists on both sides of the dividing line and the "wall of shame."

Throughout Eastern Europe, the Communist regimes have become more relaxed, less monolithic, less uniquely centered on Moscow. This post-Stalinist policy has given Moscow many problems, but it has also led to a greater acceptance, albeit with little enthusiasm, of the Communist regimes in such countries as Poland, Czechoslovakia, and Roumania. It is now possible to be "more Polish," or "more Czech," or "more Roumanian," without necessarily being less Communist. Since the desire to become more Polish corresponds also with the desire of the Poles, this evolution, despite the many problems it creates for the Communist leadership, introduces an element of identity and consequent stability. At the very least, such events as the uprisings in Poland and Hungary are not likely to happen again in the foreseeable future.

This prescription does not work in East Germany. The East Germans do not want to become "more East German"; they want to become "more German." Hence any relaxation of the East German Communist regime, any concessions to popular demands that can be expressed in East Germany, will fail to achieve the results which the Communists have found elsewhere in Eastern Europe. It is no wonder, therefore, that the hated Ulbricht dictatorship clings to Stalinist methods of repression; and although many Communists recognize the need for bringing the DDR more in line with other East European countries, nobody knows exactly how to go about it without totally undermining the Communist regime. Hence a feeling of the unreal and the impermanent, and even a sentiment of isolation, abound in the DDR.

The situation is of course quite different in the Federal Republic. Here we find a normal democratic regime with free and divergent political parties, with a free press, with freedom of expression, and especially with freedom of movement. Citizens of the German Federal Republic may go where they please; nobody prevents their departure from the country, there is no "wall of shame" to keep them in, and there is no law to punish them for illegal departures.[5] And yet there is the aura of the incomplete, of the impermanent, about the Federal Republic also. In

---

[5] While the DDR Government has issued passes for special occasions and after protracted negotiations to allow West Germans, and lately West Berliners, to visit the DDR, it only rarely allows East Germans and especially East Berliners to visit the West even temporarily. See *Bundesministerium für Gesamtdeutsche Fragen, SBZ von A bis Z, ein Taschen und Nachschlagebuch über die Sowietische Besatzungszone,* Bonn, 1956, p. 217.

the opinion of a growing number of Germans, the Federal Republic is an administrative device, a necessary convenience, but not a true i.e. historical "state," especially in the emotional sense of that word. Emotionally one can be German, or even Bavarian, but not "Federal German" *(Bundesdeutsch).*

For a number of years this reality was only barely visible because of other factors. In the years immediately after World War II, German energies were primarily absorbed in the gigantic struggle for reconstruction and by the need to adjust their attitudes towards the changed world at large and towards the victorious western powers in particular. Then there was also the dream of "Europe." The idea of a United Europe was certainly not new. It finds its roots in antiquity and in the Middle Ages. During the Weimar period a number of German statesmen, especially the longtime Foreign Minister Gustav Stresemann, were the leaders of the Pan-Europe movement. But the idea received reality only after 1945 when the power centers of the world had moved away from continental Europe, thus revealing the power struggles of the past as an unending European civil war. Moreover, the influence of the Marshall Plan and the resulting necessity for European countries to pool their planning and resources, and last but not least the presence of outstanding Europeans (especially Robert Schuman and Jean Monnet of France, Paul-Henri Spaak of Belgium, Konrad Adenauer of Germany, and Alcide de Gasperi of Italy) who understood the challenge and the opportunities of the time gave the idea of a more united Europe at last a beginning and a reality in the forms of the European Coal and Steel Community (Schuman Plan), the European Atomic Energy Community (EURATOM), and the European Economic Community (Common Market).

It has been said that the Germans became "the best Europeans" perhaps because of a reaction to the excessive nationalism of the past, or perhaps because they saw in it the possibility of their final rehabilitation. Or there may have been other reasons, but there is no doubt that the idea of a united Europe was very popular in Germany. It was perhaps relative inexperience in political matters in the German body politic that created excessive hopes for early establishment of a united Europe. At any rate, for a while "Europe" served as a substitute fatherland.

Largely, though not exclusively, as a result of the anti-integrationist conviction and acts of France's President de Gaulle, these perhaps excessive hopes lost some of their flavor and reality and a now more sceptical generation poses once again the question of its identity. To an increasing extent Germans find it difficult to see this identity in either East or West Germany but find it only in "Germany," or, if that were possible, in Europe.

Hence German reunification, or perhaps more accurately the thinking about German reunification, has become a German national necessity to which no politician can long remain indifferent. Coupled with this runs the fear that unless the thought of reunification is constantly kept alive, the two Germanies will inevitably grow farther away from each other. To some extent this has already happened. True, the Communist tyrants of the DDR have only an infinitesimal following. During occasional visits in the West, East German officials, sometimes under the influence of the famous German beer, have admitted that in any really free elections they would be speedily and overwhelmingly swept out of office. Nevertheless, East Germany is a very different country now. The Communist environment and education have taken their toll, not so much in making people Communists—in that they have failed—but in changing their thinking in many ways. If one talks to East Germans of proven anti-Communist leanings, one finds that they will frequently fall into a Communist vocabulary or speak of the "achievements" (*Errungenschaften*) of the DDR even though they may mean nothing more than a social security system the like of which may be found in any number of Western countries. Also the picture which even East German anti-Communists have of the world has been affected by the constant drumming of Communist propaganda.

Thus two factors, the relatively recent awakening from the dream that an integrated Europe was an imminent development, and the fear that the separation of the two Germanies is progressing rapidly, have combined to create a sense of urgency and have made German reunification a primary political factor. It has been said often that many West Germans, being wealthy and self-satisfied, merely pay lip-service to reunification while secretly dreading the considerable financial and other sacrifices that would be necessary if the "poor cousins from the East" were to come home. This may well be true in a number of cases but politically has little significance. No German will openly oppose reunification, and a sense of solidarity or shame would probably prevent him from doing so privately. There is also a sense of responsibility, if not guilt. Most Germans realize that the division of Germany is the result of Naziism and war; but to quote the French professor Alfred Grosser, there is also the fact, perhaps unique in history, that the West Germans, when confronted with a choice between freedom and unity, did make a deliberate choice for freedom. Unity under Communism was and remains always available.

To be sure, few Germans have realistic plans for a way in which reunification could actually be achieved. Force is obviously excluded in the nuclear age for even the most rabid nationalist must recognize that in such an event there might be no Germany left to reunify; and many realize that Germany may not have enough bargaining points on her side to negotiate reunification in freedom without a broader world settlement of East-West relations, which in this magnitude does not seem very near. The Soviet Union has a strong position in East Germany. Under present and forseeable circumstances it is difficult to see what Germany could offer in return for such a concession.

From all this emerges a clear political fact: to preserve its identity, to emphasize its existence, Germany and the Germans feel compelled in those regions where they can speak freely, constantly to uphold the desire and the ideal of reunification; they must seek every opportunity to bring it into international and national discussions, and must generally keep it alive no matter how long that may take, no matter how long the realization may be delayed, even, if unhappily, it were never to be realized. From now on, this is and will remain a political fact which German political leaders and foreign statesmen dealing with Germany can forget only at their peril.

CHAPTER FIVE

The Constitutional Fabric of the German Federal Republic

GERMAN FEDERALISM has a most curious history. From 1815 to 1866 Germany, if one could regard it as a single entity at all, was a very loose confederation. The abortive revolutionary movement of 1848 and its assembly at St. Paul's Church in Frankfurt drafted the outlines of a federal constitution which never became a reality. However, it did profoundly influence the constitutions of the German Empire of 1871 and of the Weimar Republic of 1919. This draft had been greatly influenced by the Constitution of the United States, but when that was applied to the German realities, considerable differences occurred. The constitutional life of the United States contains federal and state authorities with their sometimes separate, sometimes overlapping, jurisdictions existing side by side. The German Constitutions of 1849, 1871, 1919, and now 1949, on the other hand, completely integrated federal and State (Laender) institutions while maintaining the federal principle and, in fact, a very considerable federal reality.

Another peculiarity was the fact that the German Federation, as founded in 1871, contained an administrative monstrosity, the Land of Prussia, which comprised two-thirds of the territory of the "Federal Empire." The otherwise almost inevitable competition between federal and Prussian authorities was avoided by Bismarck's decision to fuse the two machineries to a large extent by making the Prussian bureaucracy and administration the core of the federal administrative machinery. In 1919 this was no longer possible, and growing difficulties occurred when the political composition of Prussia and of the Federal Republic no longer coincided.

Prussia disappeared as a single administrative unit, not at the end of the war as might be supposed, but already in 1944 when the Nazi regime, pursuing its centralist tendencies, abolished the last remaining Prussian office, the then wholly nominal position of Minister President of Prussia, occupied by Marshal Hermann Goering who was also Reich Minister for Air. This did not much matter for the Allied occupation authorities would have abolished it anyway, in principle because much of the evil which had spawned Naziism had been attributed to Prussian influence (often incorrectly), and practically because Germany's division into zones of occupation made the preservation of a Land, which reached from the French to the Polish frontiers, totally impossible.

The abolition of Prussia made it possible after World War II to construct a federal union whose component parts were more nearly comparable in size and population, although, unavoidably, considerable inequalities remained. For a variety of motives a distinctly federal regime was agreed to by nearly all. Among the occupation authorities the French (unlike their own preference at home) favored extreme federalism for Germany in order to weaken central authority as far as possible. The Americans favored federalism out of a somewhat exaggerated faith in the identification of federalism with democracy.

The majority of the German members of the Parliamentary Council, especially the Christian Democratic Union, stood for federalism and preferred to see the new Germany appear as the successor of the 1848 tradition. Among German parties, only the Social Democratic Party stood for more centralist tendencies, and this was a matter of principle rather than of practical politics. The Parliamentary Council, which had the task of drafting the "basic law," was composed of members of the Laender parliaments, some of whom had already adopted constitutions, such as Bavaria and Hesse (1946), Bremen and Rhineland-Palatinate (1947). The draft which the Parliamentary Council was to prepare had to be ratified by at least two-thirds of the Laender parliaments. A centralist constitution could hardly have emerged under such circumstances.

Perhaps the Constitution would have provided for an even more decentralized regime had it not been for an interesting episode of far-reaching consequence. The reader will recall that the new Constitution and the Occupation Statute were tied together, and that the occupying powers had reserved very extensive powers to themselves. This had aroused the particular opposition of the Social Democrats and especially of their leader, the late Dr. Kurt Schumacher. It soon became clear that a majority for a draft text would be possible only if the occupying powers were to reduce their claims. At a dramatic moment Dr. Schumacher declared, "Either there is going to be German cooperation or we shall have a foreign law imposed on Germany by superior might." The Allied Powers gave in sufficiently to make a majority possible, but the Schumacher influence created a more centralist document than might otherwise have been the case.

Demonstrative of both the federal and "provisional" character of the Constitution was the peculiar choice of a small university city, Bonn, as the capital. Since Berlin was out of the question, Frankfurt would have seemed to have the best claim, especially as it had already been the headquarters of the bizonal administration and was one of the most important and most centrally located cities of the new Republic. But Frankfurt was located in the *Land* of Hesse whose Social Democratic majority did not please the Christian Democratic majority in the Parliamentary Council. Possibly even more decisive was the fact that the Parliamentary Council's dominant personality and the great architect of the Federal Republic, Dr. Konrad Adenauer, had his home in Rhoendorf near Bonn, on the opposite side of the Rhine. It is difficult to think of a less suitable place as a capital of the dynamic Federal Republic than this little town, to which Germans frequently refer as the "federal village." But its very unsuitability was in fact also an argument in its favor because it demonstrated the provisional character of the Federal Republic which the members of the Parliamentary Council wished so strongly to underline.

The major territorial subdivisions of the German Federal Republic are traditionally called *Land* (plural: *Laender*). The first impression of the Federal-Laender relationship would seem to weigh things very much in favor of the central power. This impression is heightened by the fact that of the present Laender, only Bavaria and the Hanseatic cities of Hamburg and Bremen have separate historical identities. North Rhine Westphalia, Schleswig-Holstein, and the Saarland were remnants of Prussia, which is also true of parts of Lower Saxony, Rhineland Palatinate, and Hesse. Artificial is also the combined Land of Baden-Wuertemberg. But a closer look at the constitutional and administrative, and also the political realities indicates very considerable powers of the Laender.

By far the biggest *Land* in population is North Rhine Westphalia with nearly 16 million inhabitants, although in area Bavaria is largest with over 27 thousand square miles. The smallest *Land* in both population and area is Bremen with slightly over 700 thousand inhabitants and 156 square miles.

The Basic Law has adopted the principle of the American Constitution by which the powers of the federal government are expressed and enumerated while those of the Laender are residual. Exclusive federal control extends to foreign affairs, nationality, passports, migration and extradition, currency, customs, border control, railroad and air traffic, post and telegraph, trade mark and copyright legislation. To these were added in 1954, defense, military conscription, and civil defense. The federal government also has exclusive right of legislation over the form of cooperation between federal and Laender governments in matters concerning criminal police, the protection of the Constitution, and international cooperation in the fight against crime (Art. 73).

The field of concurrent powers in which both the federal government and the Laender may legislate is far more extensive. It covers the entire economy, all criminal and civil law as well as all labor legislation, the control of associations and assemblies, of railway, highway and water traffic, and many more subjects too numerous to mention (Art. 74). Only education and practically all police business remain exclusively in the hands of the Laender. However, "in order to avert imminent danger to the existence of the free democratic basic order of the Federal Union or a Land, a Land may call for police assistance from other Laender." But if the Land concerned is not in a position to combat that danger, "the Federal Government may place the police in that Land, or the police forces of other Laender under its control" (Art. 91). This arrangement must be rescinded after the danger has passed or whenever the *Bundesrat* (Federal Council) demands it.

The Constitution attempts to establish limits to federal legislation by the provision (Art. 72) that there shall be federal legislation in the area of concurrent powers only under the following conditions:

1. when a matter cannot be effectively regulated by the Laender;
2. if the regulations of one Land prejudice the rights of another Land or Laender;
3. if "the preservation of legal or economic unity demands in particular the preservation of uniformity of living conditions extending beyond the territory of an individual Land."

Considerable potential power is alsno vested in the federal government through the integration of federal and Land bureaucracies. With certain exceptions, the federal authorities do not maintain regional or local offices of their own, and rely on the administrative services of the Laender and their subdivisions to execute federal law and regulations, (as explained fully in the section on the Federal Administration). Thus the Laender bureaucracies have two sets of functions: those which they exercise in their "autonomous" role, and those which devolve upon them in their "derivative" role as regional and local agencies of the federal government. This makes a certain amount of federal control inevitable and the Basic Law provides that the federal government shall exercise supervision over the governments of the Laender to the extent of seeing to it that the federal laws are faithfully executed. The federal government may also establish uniform standards and practices for the conduct of the administrative services, and may even send supervisory commissioners to the Laender governments with the permission of those governments themselves or with that of the Federal Council. The federal government may also issue specific orders pertaining to single cases (*Einzelanweisungen*).

Under the Weimar Constitution, the Reich government had the right to compel the Laender to obedience even by the use of armed force. The Basic Law of the new Federal Republic is more circumspect. Article 37 provides that if a *Land* does not fulfill its obligations under the Constitution or under the federal law, the federal government may compel obedience by all means at its disposal and may also commandeer or direct the facilities of the Laender. This is called "federal compulsion" (*Bundeszwang*). However, in contrast to the Weimar regime, such action is possible only with the consent of the Federal Council. It is also possible for a Land or for the federal government to lodge a complaint with the Federal Council charging a Land with the non-fulfillment of its obligations in those fields in which the federal government, under the Constitution, has a right of supervision. The Federal Council then may decide with finality (Art. 84) what should be done. In either case, however, the Land concerned can appeal to the Federal Constitutional Court; also both the federal government or any one of the Laender may directly sue a Land before the Federal Constitutional Court for the nonfulfillment of its duties.

Of special significance are the fiscal authorities. The centralist tendencies of the Constitution are in evidence in the system by which the federal authorities have principal responsibility for the collection of all taxes. These in turn are then redistributed by a form of equalization (*Finanzausgleich*) which places major responsibility in the hands of the federal government. The Constitution provides in great detail which taxes and revenues belong exclusively to the federal government, which belong to the Laender, and which are in the joint domain. The more important taxes, such as income taxes, are collected centrally and distributed according to a complicated equalization system roughly in the proportion of one-third to the federal government and two-thirds to the Laender. It is then up to the Laender to decide by Land law the amount of their income to devolve on the municipal administrations. But if all sources of public income are taken into consideration, the picture is reversed: thus for the fiscal year 1960, the federal authorities received 53.3 percent, the Laender 31.3 percent, the municipalities 12.4 percent, while 3 percent was reserved for the "equalization of burdens fund."[1]

[1] The so-called "equalization of burdens fund" (*Lastenausgleichsfonds*) took cognizance of the fact that the care for refugees and expellees, aid and compensation for war damage, various kinds of pensions and compensations for losses incurred by victims of the Nazi regime, imposed exceptionally heavy burdens on the federal government.

This system is not intrinsically unfair as the federal government has had to shoulder exceptionally heavy expenses, first with regard to the enormous influx of refugees and expellees, and later in the field of national defense. It is, however, difficult to administer and requires complicated agreements which sometimes materialize only as a result of prolonged annual negotiations.

Although the system appears to be heavily weighted in the direction of the federal government, the appearance is somewhat misleading because of the central role played by the Federal Council (*Bundesrat*). As will be seen in greater detail later on, the Federal Council is not an upper house of the national legislature as is the case with the Senate of the United States, but is a council of ambassadors of the Laender governments. Members of the Federal Council are not elected. They are appointed by the Laender governments, are subject to instructions from them, and are subject to recall. In all matters of legislation concerning federal relationships, the Federal Council has an absolute veto: in other types of legislation it may be over-ruled by the lower house, the *Bundestag*. This is also true regarding amendments to the federal Constitution, because the Laender governments have such an important role to play in all aspects of federal legislation and even administration. Laender elections have become permeated by national issues as the federal government tries to obtain the strongest possible support in the *Bundesrat*. However, even to the extent that it has been successful—and it has never been completely successful—Laender governments dominated by a particular political party have not always toed the line of that same party on the national level when "state's rights" were involved. Hence, federalism has found a very substantial bulwark in the Federal Council. Nor should the role of the Federal Constitutional Court be overlooked. When the federal government made some tentative gestures towards establishing a (second) system of radio and television networks, the Court decreed a determined halt. This has forced the Laender to organize regional associations in order to get this program underway.

Of exceptional importance is the near total authority of the Laender regarding all levels of education. If it is nevertheless true that the German educational system is today following more unified principles than has ever been the case before, this is largely due to the excellent work of the "Conference of Ministers of Education" which has attempted with considerable success to standardize the German educational system on all levels without weakening the principle of *Land* control. By and large this system has worked very well, because it has enabled various Laender to pioneer in many aspects of education and training. More progress has probably been achieved in this manner than if the ponderous federal machinery had to be set in motion. At the same time, a healthy competition between the universities and other educational institutions of the various Laender has undoubtedly added to the speed with which they have made a very appreciable comeback from the ravages of the Nazi and war periods.

But the "economic miracle" has made it possible for many more young men and women to enroll in the universities. In the spring semester of 1963, 234,105 students (not counting 21,568 foreigners) were enrolled in German universities, an astonishingly large number when one considers that continental European universities are essentially graduate and professional schools. These students often found inadequate facilities; they found the expansion of the faculty hampered by a system in which well-established, full professors could effectively throttle the flow of newcomers when they saw fit to do so; and they found that the necessary funds for expansion were often unobtainable from the respective ministers of education. These conditions have made for sharp criticism. However, remedial measures are being planned through the creation of new universities like the one in Regensburg, and by the adoption of new types of organization as is planned for the new University of Constance.

With all its problems and especially its financial difficulties, German federalism, although substantially different from its American counterpart, constitutes a living reality which has worked with greater success than some of its critics assumed it would or could.

CHAPTER SIX

Civil Liberties

IN CONTRAST to the French Constitution of 1946 which placed civil liberties in the preamble, and in even greater contrast to that of 1958 which merely proclaimed the "attachment" of the French people to the rights of man as elaborated by the aforementioned preamble of 1946, the German Constitution places the protection of civil liberties in the constitutional text itself and most prominently, at the very beginning.

This special emphasis was intentional and was designed to underscore the contrast between the new Germany and the total disregard for personal rights which characterized the Nazi regime. This impression is further deepened by the text of Articles 1 and 2 of the Constitution which form a kind of declaration of basic values guiding the entire constitutional system. In a deliberate gesture, Article 1 begins with the declaration that the dignity of man is inviolable and that to respect and protect it is the duty of all state authority. This emphasis clearly refers back to the feature which was perhaps the most onerous of Hitler's Third Reich, namely the total disregard and contempt for human dignity exemplified by the total lawlessness of the concentration camps, or the invectives hurled at the accused by the so-called "People's Courts."

Equally basic is the declaration in Article 2 that "everyone has the right to the free development of his personality insofar as he does not violate the right of others or offend against the constitutional order or the moral code." This is an attempt to put Immanuel Kant's "categorical imperative" into the Constitution, and there would seem to be no objections to this as both Articles 1 and 2 emphasize general principles rather than strictly positive law. However, to avoid any misconception that all the civil liberties enumerated in this and other sections of the Constitution might be considered merely "declaratory," (an assertion frequently made regarding certain sections of the Weimar Constitution). Article 1, Section 3 stipulates that the basic rights listed therein "bind the legislature, the executive, and the judiciary as directly enforceable law."

The Constitution provides for the inviolability of the human person except where the law provides otherwise, as well as for the equality of men and women. The latter provision has been difficult to implement and there still is a rather general wage differential in Germany. There are the usual protections of free speech, of press, and assembly. There is also the equivalent of a habeas corpus procedure which in some respects is even more ironclad than is the case in the United States; under the provisions of Article 104 of the Constitution, a person under arrest need not apply for a writ of habeas corpus himself. The procedure is automatic. On the day following his arrest, he must be taken before a judge, who must decide. But on the other hand, under German practice, it is more difficult to be released on bail.

The provisions of Article 3, Section 3 are lucid and detailed denying discrimination or favor because of sex, heritage, race, language, homeland, origin, faith, religious or political opinion. It is difficult to see how this list could be more complete. In a positive sense Article 4 once again returns to the question of faith and conscience, declaring freedom of creed and religious or ideological views inviolable. It also guarantees an undisturbed practice of religion.

It is interesting that conscientious objection to military service was specifically guaranteed in the original version of the Constitution well before the military services were reconstituted. Further provisions pertaining thereto were contained in amendments to the Constitution enacted on March 19, 1956.

Property rights are also guaranteed but there is the usual right of the government to take private property for public use with just compensation (eminent domain). Appeal to the regular courts is permissible in case of dispute.

Somewhat unusual is the provision of Article 9 underlining a specific right to join labor unions and to outlaw agreements not to join unions (Yellow Dog contracts). There is, however, no specific mention of the right to strike.

Also of interest is the provision of Article 16 according to which no one may be deprived of his German citizenship. Loss of citizenship may arise only pursuant to a law; and if against the will of the person affected, only if such person does not thereby become stateless. This unusually elaborate provision is explained by the practices of the Nazi regime which withdrew German citizenship from politically and racially persecuted groups. Also in the same Article is a provision which appears strange to the Anglo-American legal tradition: no German citizen may be extradited to a foreign power. This has been taken over from the Weimar Constitution and has been justified by the fact that German criminal law permits German courts to try citizens for offences committed abroad. However, the implementation of this provision is often difficult and may in effect grant a right to asylum when none was intended. In this connection, it is useful to point out that the provision "abroad" (*an das Ausland*) does not cover East Germany, the so-called "German Democratic Republic," which the Constitution and the laws of the Federal Republic treat as an integral part of Germany.

The constitutional legal provisions regarding education are unusual. Article 7 of the Constitution stipulates in Section 1 that "the entire educational system is under the supervision of the state." However, the word state (*Staat*) is in this case not a reference to federal or Land authority in particular but to public authority in general. Actually the Constitution leaves no doubt that no part of education is under federal authority, and the provisions of Article 7 merely lays down certain ground rules which the Laender have to observe. This rather unusual formulation was the result of deep differences in the Parliamentary Council reflecting the sensitivity of religious questions in Germany. The Constitution guarantees that religious instruction is given in all schools as one of the regular subjects and that the principles of such instructions are to be determined by the churches concerned. Only the so-called "nonconfessional schools" are exempt. Otherwise the rule applies to all schools public or private. In each case it is the right of the parent or guardian to determine whether minor children are to attend religious instruction or not.

Because religious instruction is given in public schools (except in Bremen), and because in certain Laender, such as Bavaria,

Catholic schools may also be public schools, the need for private schools is limited. The Constitution permits their establishment but requires that a need for their existence be shown and that they meet the same standards as public schools. Particularly interesting is the provision which prohibits the licensing of private schools when there is "a segregation of the pupils according to the means of the parents," or if the "economic or legal position of the teaching staff is not sufficiently assured." Also rather stringent is the provision that private elementary schools shall be permitted only if the authorities concerned find that they serve "a special pedagogic interest, or if parents request the establishment of a religious or nonreligious school and that type of school does not already exist in the community."

The memory of Germany's recent past was also clearly expressed in the provision of the Constitution that "art and science, research and teaching are free." But the very next sentence reminds one of the abuses of the universities by the Nazis even before they came to power, for it reads: "the freedom of teaching does not absolve from a duty of loyalty to the Constitution." Naturally these provisions regarding academic freedom and its limitation through loyalty to the Constitution refer only to institutions of higher education. In primary and secondary schools, teaching follows prescribed rules laid down by competent authority as it does everywhere else.

The theory and practice of every democratic country has had to come to the conclusion that there are no "unlimited rights." The Supreme Court of the United States has had numerous occasions to identify such conclusions. The modification has been indicated in several instances by the reference in the German Constitution that "certain rights could be exercised within the framework of the law." This was criticized when used under the Weimar Constitution because civil rights are actually endangered in exceptional and critical times when legislatures can become rubber stamps for governmental power. The Bonn Constitution attempts to prevent abuses in several ways. In the first place it declares all basic rights directly binding upon all courts and authorities. Second, the Law Creating the Federal Constitutional Court of March 12, 1951, also permits individuals whose civil rights have been violated to make a direct demand for redress

(*Verfassungsbeschwerde*) to the Federal Constitutional Court. Third, it is stipulated that limitations of basic rights by law must be general and must not apply to specific cases only. The basic nature of the civil right must not be changed. These are not absolute safeguards but so far the record is quite good.

Highly controversial on the other hand is Article 18, which provides that

. . . whoever abuses freedom of expression of opinion, in particular freedom of the press, freedom of teaching, freedom of assembly, freedom of association, the secrecy of mail, post and telecommunications, property, or the right of asylum, in order to attack the free democratic basic order, forfeits these basic rights. The forfeiture and its extent are pronounced by the Federal Constitutional Court.

Article 21 furthermore declares, in Section 2

. . . parties which, by reason of their aims or the behavior of their adherents, seek to impair or destroy the free democratic basic order or to endanger the existence of the Federal Republic of Germany are unconstitutional. The Federal Constitutional Court decides on the question of unconstitutionality.

The definition of just what constitutes a "misuse" by individuals runs into almost insurmountable difficulties, especially as the "forfeiture" of these rights does not constitute a penalty under the law. Certainly the line is difficult to draw between the exercise of the extensive rights guaranteed in the Constitution and the concept of abuse.

More concrete in its importance has been the provision in Article 21, Section 2, regarding the suppression of undemocratic parties. Here two actual instances have occurred, namely the suppression of a neo-Nazi group known as the Socialist Reich Party, and the suppression of the Communist Party. We shall discuss some of the criteria employed by the court when we examine the Federal Constitutional Court. However, one peculiar detail of the Federal Constitutional Court's decision regarding the suppression of the Communist Party is noteworthy. The verdict confined the application of the decree dissolving the Communist Party to the area actually governed by the basic law (*nur für den vom Grundgesetz zeitlich und sachlich beherrschten Raum*), meaning the Federal Republic. This constitutes a departure from the general legal assumption that the basic law applies to all Germany including Eastern Germany even though it can of course not be executed there. The specific exemption of this decision's application to Eastern Germany was motivated by the wish to avoid any obstacle to future all-German elections where parties now suppressed in West Germany might nevertheless, for political reasons, have to be admitted.

Sufficient time has not elapsed to permit definitive judgment of the record of the safeguard of civil liberties in the Federal Republic. But it is clear that the fathers of the Constitution were mindful both of the need to protect these rights and of the bitter experience of abuses which went rampant under the Weimar Constitution that proved powerless to prevent anti-democratic and anti-constitutional organizations from turning it against itself. In making the Federal Constitutional Court the guardian of civil rights, the Constitution established important safeguards. The Court has proven itself to be both courageous, outspoken, and independent.

Political Parties in the BUNDESTAG from 1949 to 1965

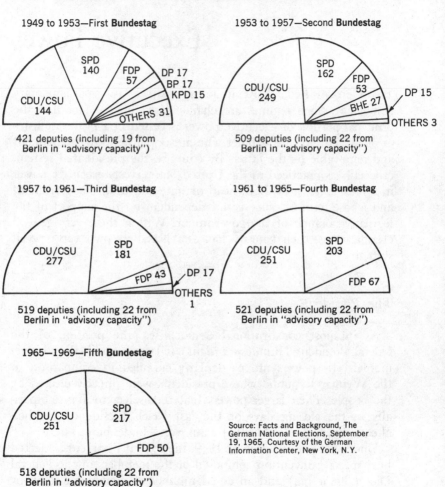

1949 to 1953—First **Bundestag**

SPD 140
FDP 57
CDU/CSU 144
DP 17
BP 17
KPD 15
OTHERS 31

421 deputies (including 19 from Berlin in "advisory capacity")

1953 to 1957—Second **Bundestag**

SPD 162
FDP 53
CDU/CSU 249
BHE 27
DP 15
OTHERS 3

509 deputies (including 22 from Berlin in "advisory capacity")

1957 to 1961—Third **Bundestag**

CDU/CSU 277
SPD 181
FDP 43
DP 17
OTHERS 1

519 deputies (including 22 from Berlin in "advisory capacity")

1961 to 1965—Fourth **Bundestag**

CDU/CSU 251
SPD 203
FDP 67

521 deputies (including 22 from Berlin in "advisory capacity")

1965—1969—Fifth **Bundestag**

CDU/CSU 251
SPD 217
FDP 50

518 deputies (including 22 from Berlin in "advisory capacity")

Source: Facts and Background, The German National Elections, September 19, 1965, Courtesy of the German Information Center, New York, N.Y.

CHAPTER SEVEN

Executive Power

THE German Federal Republic is classified as a parliamentary democracy. Such regimes are characterized by the fact that the principal portion of executive power is vested in a prime minister or chancellor and his cabinet who are responsible to a parliament and removable by the latter. By contrast, the presidential system, especially as practiced in the United States, vests executive power in a president who is both head of state and head of government and whose term of office is not dependent on the support of the legislative branch of the government. Within these very general classifications, each country has established its own very special system.

The President

As in most constitutional democracies, the position of the federal President (*Bundespräsident*) is largely nominal and ceremonial. His powers are particularly curtailed in comparison to the Weimar Republic whose presidents were directly elected by the people. Their larger powers lent themselves to abuse, especially in the closing days of the last Reich President, the then already senile Field Marshal Paul von Hindenburg.

Under the Constitution of 1949, the federal President is elected by a special convention composed of the members of the Federal Diet (*Bundestag*) and an equal number of members elected by the legislatures of the Laender according to the principle of proportional representation. The term of the President is five years, one more than that of the *Bundestag*. He may be re-elected only once. If the President is incapacitated or if the office becomes prematurely vacant, its functions are temporarily exercised by the

President of the upper house, the Federal Council (*Bundesrat*). In case the President dies in office, new elections are held within thirty days after his demise.

The fact that the President's powers are more nominal than real is underlined by the provision of the Constitution which requires that all his acts be countersigned either by the federal Chancellor or by a cabinet minister. Under those circumstances, the Chancellor and the Ministers rather than the President assume responsibility. Theoretically, under Article 58 of the Constitution, no countersignature is required when the President nominates or dismisses the Federal Chancellor. However, this is wholly theoretical. As we shall see, a Chancellor who is designated by the President must still be elected by the Diet, which means that the President can in fact nominate only a man who has the confidence of the majority of the legislature, and it is that majority rather than the President which makes the real choice. Nor is the dismissal power anything but nominal because the President would find his position untenable if he were to exercise it. In reality a Chancellor's term will end by death or resignation, and nominally too at the end of each legislative term of the parliament. If the President were to dismiss the Chancellor who still commands a majority in parliament, the latter would simply refuse to re-elect any other person, and the President would find himself in an impossible position. The exercise of the dismissal power is therefore unthinkable under all foreseeable circumstances.

Compared to the positions of other heads of state, whether monarchs or presidents in parliamentary democracies, the powers of the German federal President are among the least important. And yet, the position of the federal presidency has achieved considerable significance in another way. This was primarily the work of the first President of the new Federal Republic, the late Dr. Theodor Heuss. This former professor and leader of the Free Democratic Party, a moderate and liberal in every sense of that term, and a man of deep culture, gave his office a style and a dignity which proved highly significant. On one or two occasions President Heuss was perhaps ill-advised to try to assert himself, as for instance in December, 1952, when he requested an opinion by the Federal Constitutional Court about the constitutionality of the European Defense Community Treaty; this was a project for the establishment of a European Defense Community (EDC) that attempted to create an integrated European army. It was defeated in the French National Assembly in 1954. No doubt President Heuss had that right, but the request dealing with a highly controversial subject was capable of being interpreted as a partisan-like interference, and Chancellor Adenauer succeeded in dissuading President Heuss from pursuing this course of action. President Heuss withdrew his request one hour before the Federal Constitutional Court was to announce its decision.

But these incidents were quickly forgotten under the impression made by the profound humanity and simplicity of the President. At a time when both democracy and the republican institutions of the country were fragile and untested, he appealed to the conscience of his fellow citizens with great and stirring effect. His speeches, which he wrote himself without exception, were literary and intellectual masterpieces, frequently exhibiting great courage and straightforwardness. Thus he became a symbol of unity and contributed greatly to the maturing and the stability of the Federal Republic. At his first election in 1949, the leader of the Social Democratic opposition insisted on a nominal opposing candidacy on the first ballot. Heuss received 377 votes against Schumacher's 311 (402 was the required majority), and he was elected on the second ballot with 416 votes. But at his second election in 1954, President Heuss had become the universally accepted symbol of the nation and was re-elected on the first ballot by 871 votes out of 987.

The election of President Heuss's successor, Dr. Heinrich Luebke, in 1959 was again opposed because of the maneuvers of Chancellor Adenauer and the widespread resistance thereto. Undoubtedly the fact that the candidate of the Social Democratic opposition, Dr. Carlo Schmid, seemed to many members of the Federal Assembly to be a man more in the style of President Heuss, also contributed to the split vote.

It is significant, however, that when President Luebke was up for re-election in 1964, the leadership of the Social Democratic opposition decided, against considerable opposition in their own ranks, to vote for Luebke's re-election in order to demonstrate the basic unity of the country.

Although President Heinrich Luebke has not attained the style

and universal popularity of his predecessor, and has therefore
been the object of some criticism, his impartiality and devotion
to duty as well as his attachment to the democratic institutions
of the country have been beyond reproach and have in no small
manner contributed to the decision of the Social Democratic
Party to support his re-election.

The Chancellor and his Cabinet

A description and analysis of the key position in the German
governmental structure, the Chancellorship, must blend constitutional provisions, political reality, and personalities. At the
closing of 1965, the Federal Republic has had only two Chancellors, Dr. Konrad Adenauer and Dr. Ludwig Erhard. Both men
headed cabinets based on the same coalition and in the main
composed of the same persons. Their majorities also were the
same until September, 1965. Both men had strong positions. Yet
their styles and manner of execution are almost as different as
night and day. To some extent this comparison permits us to
separate the office from the man—only to note that it is after all
the man as well as political realities which determine the final
outcome.

The Basic Law was intended to guard against the instability and
the frequent cabinet crises which had marked the history of the
Weimar Republic. When the Constitution of 1949 was written,
it was not as yet known whether the Federal Republic would
again develop the debilitating over-proliferation of parties which
characterized the Weimar period or whether it would in fact
move toward a two-party system. Hence the Constitution was
designed to make frivolous over-throw of cabinets as difficult as
possible. It provides that the Chancellor, and he alone, is nominated by the President and that he must be elected without
debate by the lower house, the *Bundestag*. In a multi-party system
where combinations and different majorities are possible, the
federal President might have some influence in the choice of the
Chancellor-designate, as was the case both under the Weimar
Republic and in the Third and Fourth French Republics. However, under the near-two-party system which has developed in

Germany, the outcome of the election, as in Great Britain, actually determines the person of the future Chancellor. This means in fact that the political parties designate and the voters appoint the Chancellor; or where a coalition is involved, the informal negotiations among the coalition party leaders determine in effect the person of the man whom the President must nominate and who will then be elected.

If the person so nominated is not elected, the *Bundestag* may, two weeks later, elect a federal Chancellor without presidential nomination. In either case, a majority of all members of the *Bundestag*, whether present or not, is required. If this still does not produce a Chancellor, another ballot is taken in which plurality suffices. The federal President must appoint a Chancellor who has been elected by majority whether nominated by the President or not. However, a Chancellor-designate who has been elected only by plurality, confronts the President with one of his few real choices; he can either appoint him or dissolve the parliament and call for new elections. But, as Germany appears to move more and more toward a two-party system, such a situation is most unlikely to occur.

It should be noted that the other members of the cabinet are not elected; the Chancellor proposes their appointment and the President has no choice but to comply. The Constitution provides that the Chancellor alone determines the general lines of policy and that he alone bears responsibility for them. This is also underlined by the fact that a vote of confidence or censure is introduced by, or directed against, the Chancellor and its outcome determines the fate of the cabinet.

In actuality, however, it is political reality, rather than the constitutional text, which determines the strength with which the Chancellor leads. It is true that he nominates and in fact appoints the ministers, but unless he has the necessary agreement with his coalition partners if there is a coalition government, or with his own party if there is a one party cabinet, the nomination and appointment would not carry much reality. Even so strong a leader as Adenauer had periods of considerable delay before a government could be formed.

An interesting provision of the Constitution stipulates that a vote of nonconfidence against a government does not automatically bring the cabinet down but functions only if the *Bundestag* is able to elect a successor to the federal Chancellor by an absolute majority of its members. This can be an important safeguard when the parties are badly splintered in the parliament and when a "negative majority of discordant elements is able to amass the votes to pass a vote of censure or to refuse a demand of confidence in the government without being able to show sufficient unity to elect a successor." The Weimar period recalls instances in which both Nazis and Communists as well as other extremists assaulted a government without being able to propose alternatives. In the first parliament of the Federal Republic, when Adenauer was elected by a majority of one vote, it appeared as if this provision (Article 67) were to assume significance. This has, however, not been the case and the article has never been tested thus far. Equivalent provisions in the Laender constitutions, however, did not prevent a change when the parties who wished to effect a change had the votes and prepared their ground in advance.

Another variation is the right of the Chancellor to ask for a vote of confidence, and upon having it refused by a majority of the *Bundestag*, propose to the President the dissolution of parliament and new elections. The *Bundestag* can stop this procedure, however, by electing a new Chancellor—who could be the same one, for that matter. Technically the President could refuse the request for dissolution, but in that case the Chancellor would resign and dissolution and new elections would become inevitable in any case. Hence in reality the choice does not exist, as far as the President is concerned.

A most peculiar and involved provision of the Constitution is contained in Article 81. We have already seen that the Chancellor has at least two options when he requests a vote of confidence from the *Bundestag* and is refused. He may resign or he may cause dissolution and general elections. Article 81 gives him a third possibility. He may request the President to proclaim "a state of legislative emergency" (*Gesetzgebungsnotstand*). We shall see later, when we discuss the legislative process, how this uncommon procedure works. Suffice it to say at this time that this is yet another provision which envisages the possibility of the kind of badly split parliament which characterized the Weimar Republic and which made orderly legislation impossible for long periods. This provision is designed to make it possible in such an unsettled situation to pass at least those measures which are vitally necessary for the conduct of orderly government. However, in the political atmosphere of the Federal Republic, it is difficult to envisage a situation in which this paragraph might become operative.

Constitutionally the leadership of the Chancellor rests on Article 65 which provides that "the Federal Chancellor determines, and is responsible for, general policy." This may or may not leave a great deal of leeway because the same article also says that "each Federal Minister conducts the business of his department autonomously and on his own responsibility," and further states that "the Federal Cabinet decides on differences of opinion between Federal Ministers."

If the Constitution lays the foundation for what has come to be called "Chancellor democracy" or "Chancellor government," it became reality as a result of the extraordinary personality and style of the Federal Republic's first Chancellor, Dr. Konrad Adenauer. In the first place, he combined the position of Chancellor with the chairmanship and actual direction of the largest party, the Christian Democratic Union. Second, as Chancellor, he was the real leader and not a *"primus inter pares."* Third, his enormous popularity and his great achievements both in Germany and in the free world, the place which he had earned in the concert of nations for a country recently so despised, discredited, and destroyed went well beyond the economic sphere in what has come to be the economic miracle of Germany.

Adenauer managed to combine the authentic style of authority and virtually sovereign leadership with an equally genuine popular touch. Added to this came the experience of a long life, and a degree of physical and mental alertness despite his great age which seemed to defy the laws of nature. Perhaps most decisive was that instinct, that almost automatic appraisal of a tactical situation coupled with very definite long-range objectives, which marks the great politician and the great statesman. Controversial as were many Adenauer decisions, especially towards the end of his Chancellorship and thereafter, his genuine achievements for

Germany and the West are such that history is bound to reserve an important and honorable place for him.

Adenauer's style and virtually total control of the executive branch made it possible for him to rule in a manner very much his own. The Vice-Chancellors of his cabinets were always modest and self-effacing men—and had to be. He was not one to share power. His most intimate collaborators were not vice-chancellors or other ministers but members of his own staff, among them in particular his exceptionally able first two State Secretaries, Dr. Otto Lenz and Dr. Hans Globke. The latter certainly came closer to being a Vice-Chancellor in fact than any Vice-Chancellor by title. When Adenauer was on vacation at one of his two favorite spots, at the Buegenstock in Switzerland or at Caddenabbia in Italy, there was such a coming and going of cabinet ministers and high officials that there were even protests in Switzerland against the "use of a Swiss resort as a provisional German seat of government."

Although the Constitution provides that a minister should be autonomous in his field, Adenauer did not hesitate to intervene wherever and whenever he considered it necessary. The various lobbies and representatives of special interests, whether they were federations of industry, of labor unions, of the peasants' federation, etc., were not slow in catching on. Rather than being satisfied with seeing the cabinet minister of their particular sphere of interest, they insisted on seeing the Chancellor and were in fact encouraged by him to do so. The resultant decisions or commitments then had to be carried out by the ministers concerned. This increased the impression that the ministers were mere "secretaries" of the Chancellor. But one must also recognize that Adenauer managed this style by concentrating on questions of general policy and basic decisions and did not bother his collaborators and ministers with constant interference in the details of their work. This too is a quality which marks the outstanding leader. As is often the case with strong men, it was also a fact that the farther the field from the Chancellor's personal interest, the more independence was given the minister in charge.

Konrad Adenauer's grip on the German government loosened somewhat after 1961, as was related in the section on Political

Parties. As we have seen, his maneuvers to keep his eventual successor, Dr. Ludwig Erhard, from attaining the Chancellorship, led to a prolonged crisis that made the formation of his last cabinet a very long-drawn-out and painful affair. Finally, in order to be able to form it, Adenauer had to promise to give up the Chancellorship. This he managed to postpone until October 15, 1963, when he at last resigned at the age of 87.

All this served to make more difficult the role of his successor, Ludwig Erhard, who achieved the pinnacle of power after a long period during which he was systematically disparaged and sometimes humiliated by Adenauer. Chancellor Erhard has also had to accept other handicaps. Adenauer, retaining the position of Party Chairman, remained as a powerful counterpoise. The leader of the Free Democratic Party, Erich Mende, joined the cabinet as Vice-Chancellor with the clear intention that his party should play a stronger and more independent role than it had been able to do under Adenauer. At the same time, a new and powerful opposition group emerged within the Christian Democratic Union and especially in its Bavarian sister party, the Christian Social Union whose chairman, former Defense Minister Franz Josef Strauss, took a stand that sometimes seemed even more "oppositionist" than that of the official opposition, the Social Democratic Party.

Especially in foreign affairs Chancellor Erhard did not have the powerful position or international reputation of his predecessor, and it is particularly in that field that he and his Foreign Minister, Dr. Gerhard Schroeder, have come in for concentrated attacks.

Nevertheless, the very difficulties under which Chancellor Erhard had to hold his office, especially until the 1965 elections, made it possible to see that the office remains very strong indeed. Erhard is no more run by others than was Adenauer. Nor is he simply a presiding officer in the cabinet. Confronted by numerous rebellions, especially within his own party, he mastered them one by one although the opposition remained strong and gave every indication of wishing to return to the fray. The general determination of policy is in the hands of the new Chancellor as it was in those of the old one. Just as Adenauer had his intimate collaborators, so Erhard's Vice-Chancellor in fact but not in rank

is his Minister of State, Dr. Ludger Westrick, who was already
his right-hand man when Erhard was Minister of Economics.
In fact, it might be said that Westrick, who is sometimes called
the Sherman Adams of the German government, is even more
firmly in the saddle than was Globke.

There is no question as to who is boss. The Chancellor cannot
be outvoted in the cabinet meeting, unless he permits such a
course. This is quite unlikely and was unthinkable under Adenauer also. Moreover, the resignation of the Chancellor brings
down the entire cabinet, for he alone is elected by the *Bundestag*
and the other cabinet members obtain their positions legally from
that fact. Moreover, an attempt to outvote a Chancellor would
reveal such inner division and rivalry within the majority party
or within the ruling coalition as to make prospects dubious for
the formation of another government.

Thus rebellious cabinet ministers are likely to look before they
leap. Individual ministers of course resign from time to time as
they find their views incompatible with those of the Chancellor,
but a general revolt in the cabinet is unlikely. The customary
and richly varied forms on pressure on the Chancellor are of
course constantly in evidence, but once the Chancellor has made
up his mind, his decision stands. A good illustration of this fact
is Chancellor Erhard's insistence on keeping his embattled Foreign Minister Gerhard Schroeder who, despite an impressive performance, is not exactly popular in his own party.

Both Chancellors Adenauer and Erhard have clearly demonstrated the Chancellor's preeminence, which must therefore be
accepted as a constitutional and political fact. Different as are
their styles and interests, they have shown the Chancellorship
to be one of the strongest positions in any democratic country
in the West. The authoritative view of Professor Eschenburg
sums up the situation in these penetrating lines:

Regardless of whether the Chancellor determines the guidelines for
policy himself or takes them over from others, whether he accepts
the majority view of the Cabinet or overturns it—it is always he
alone who bears responsibility. If the Chancellor is outvoted (in
the Cabinet) he must, symbolically, withdraw from the Cabinet
meeting into his study in order once again to decide for himself and
that decision is then final. "Lonely decisions" are not merely to be
attributed to the peculiarity of Adenauer but Article 65 of the Basic

Law virtually asks for them: it is true that there has to be first deliberation and decision-making within the Cabinet as a prior step. But from the sole responsibility of the Chancellor to Parliament may be deducted the justification for these "lonely decisions." [1]

The Federal Administration

The German administrative system reflects the federal structure of the country but differs materially from that of the United States. In the latter, the federal government and each of the states maintain their own separate and complete administrative systems. Although cooperation exists on many levels and in many forms, the United States federal government does not use agents of the state governments for the administration of federal business except in certain unusual instances. Not so in Germany, as was mentioned earlier.

In the German Federal Republic, as in the Weimar Republic and in the German Empire before that, many of the federal ministries do not maintain their own branches and field agents on the Laender or local level but use directly the bureaucracy of the Laender governments and their subdivisions. Exceptions are the "classical" ministries of Foreign Affairs (which of course has no local branches), Defense and Finance (which maintain their own regional organisms). The other two "classical" ministries, Interior and Justice, do rely on Laender agencies and courts but the Ministry of the Interior does not have the central control over local and regional government which characterizes that ministry in most other European countries, especially France.

The so-called "technical" ministries are those for Post (including telephone and telegraph which are government enterprises) and Transport (which also controls the nationally owned railroad system). As in the former Reich, there are federal ministries for Economics, for Food, Agriculture and Forestry, for Labor and Social Affairs. Resulting from the special conditions after World War II, there are also ministries for Housing and for All-German Questions. The Ministry for Refugees, Escapees, and Disabled

[1] Theodor Eschenburg, *Staat und Gesellschaft in Deutschland*, Munich, Piper. 1963, p. 735.

Veterans has a declining business but the wellknown "Parkinson's Law" applies there as well, and in any case political considerations would militate against its abolition.

A special outgrowth of the federal structure is the Ministry for the Affairs of the Federal Council and of the Laender. Of growing importance is the Ministry for Science (formerly called Ministry for Nuclear Power). While the West European Union Treaty of 1954 prevents Germany from the production of nuclear weapons, it does not prohibit other nuclear research and activities, nor does it prohibit possession of nuclear weapons.

A Ministry for Family and Youth Affairs was created in 1957 largely for political reasons and to bolster the coalition structure of the government. However, since then it has done much useful work and its continued existence is not in question.

Other, somewhat specialized ministries are those for Health, for Economic Cooperation, and for Nationalized Property. For several years there has also been a Ministry for Special Tasks whose incumbent, Dr. Heinrich Krone, a senior minister, has had to undertake many important, mainly political tasks. Dr. Krone is also chairman of the National Defense Council but this is presumably an appointment which he exercises in his own right and which is not necessarily or permanently attached to the Ministry for Special Tasks. The Vice-Chancellor also serves as a kind of minister for Special Tasks but is generally assigned fewer duties especially as, in coalition government, this position has usually gone to the FDP.

There is also a special Ministry of State whose incumbent, Dr. Ludger Westrik, serves Chancellor Erhard as his right hand. But there is no Ministry for Education on the federal level, since education is strictly the affair of the Laender.

It is obvious that in Germany, as in most other countries, these ministries occupy positions of greatly varied importance, although technically they are equal. No special explanation need be given in order to show that the Foreign Ministry and the Ministry for the Affairs of the Federal Council are not on the same level. In a sense the Ministry of Finance is a kind of super-ministry, a section of which also serves as a bureau of the budget for all other ministries and government agencies.

The ministers are of course politicians and no specific professional aptitude is required of them. Nevertheless, there are certain rules of common sense which are generally observed although they are not based on statutory provisions: ministers of agriculture have invariably been former farmers or officials of agricultural associations; the minister for family affairs and youth is not likely ever to be a bachelor; nor is the minister of justice ever anything but a lawyer. The German educational system and the requirements for the public service, however, are such that candidates for ministerial posts who have professional university degrees, especially law degrees, have a much better chance than others.

The Civil Service

The German civil service has enjoyed an unusual reputation for efficiency and uncorruptibility, especially before 1914. This was the result of the traditional development of a strictly professional civil service (*Berufsbeamtentum*) and perhaps also influenced by the fact that until 1914 the basically conservative attitude of the German civil service was not considered to be a demonstration of political favoritism although one could well argue that in fact it was. The Weimar Republic saw a certain deterioration of the public service, particularly from a political point of view, when civil servants interpreted their "neutrality" in such a way that they were even neutral towards the existence and the continuation of the Republic. The Nazi regime created the greatest havoc in the public service, imposing strictly political criteria and appointing and dismissing officials on political or racial grounds. After the collapse of the Hitler regime, the public service was further thinned out through de-Nazification, and also due to the fact that between the end of the war in 1945 and the establishment of the Federal Republic in 1949, no federal service existed.

Since 1949 there has been a conscious effort to rebuild the civil service on its previous standards of excellence without returning to the remoteness and the authoritarian note which characterized it previously. A great deal of progress has been made, although some will want to argue that there is room for more. This was essentially accomplished by the Civil Service Act of 1953 which also, incidentally, nullified most of the reforms introduced under the pressure of military government and often derived from American, British, or French models.

One of the lasting characteristics of the system is that the higher civil service career remains in the main reserved to people with a legal education. This makes the system somewhat elitist, but it must be admitted that the universities have opened the door wide to thousands and thousands of students; this and the general prosperity in Germany have resulted in a considerable broadening of the base, and one can no longer say that this or any other career is confined to the sons and daughters of the upper or middle classes. Furthermore, the German universities are also public (Laender) institutions and enrollment in them is inexpensive. Also, the absence of any equivalent to the American undergraduate college means that the graduate of a law school in Germany is approximately of the same age as an American college graduate. Where the division really comes in is in the two types of secondary schools and the failure of many sons and daughters of humble homes to select the superior or academic type of secondary school which prepares for the universities. The failure to do so is almost irreparable under the German system.

There are (1963 figures) 67,255 federal and 540,238 Laender civil servants not counting judges (502 and 12,368 respectively). The German civil service is divided into four classes: the higher service (*der höhere Dienst*) for which a law degree is indispensable; the elevated service (*der gehobene Dienst*) covering responsible positions of assistantship; the middle service (*der mittlere Dienst*) comprising some assistants and slightly lower types of service; and the simple service (*der einfache Dienst*) which is largely of a menial and service nature.

Access to all of these categories, but especially to the first three, is strictly regulated on the basis of precisely defined educational prerequisites and examinations. Promotion from one group into another is possible but infrequent. The entrance examinations are controlled by commissions, but the hiring of eligible candidates is done by the government departments concerned. There is also a federal personnel commission but its sole function is quasi-judicial, that is, to grant exemptions from certain rules and to issue general regulations.

From time to time the German federal service comes under fire with accusations that religion and party membership play too great a role. Less attention is paid perhaps to a more important question about membership in, or special relations to, certain professional associations in such ministries as that for Food and Agriculture. Available data make it extremely difficult if not impossible to check on these allegations. In earlier years of the Federal Republic, when the numerical relationship between Catholics and Protestants was watched with special care, the question of religious affiliation may have played a role inasmuch as the government tried to see to it that a reasonable and equitable distribution existed. But without accurate information which would show whether church affiliations were actually used to advance one or the other career, the mere figures of a religious census within the administration would prove very little. Also, it is not illogical that relationships should exist between professional associations and civil servants within ministries dealing with the same subject matter. But cases showing that this relationship was improper and used for improper ends are very few and compare favorably with the record of other countries.

There is possibly something to the assertion that a member of the SPD is not frequently found among the highest ranking civil servants in the federal ministries. But the reverse may also be found in those city and *Land* administrations which have long been dominated by the SPD. To some extent this is the result of the fact that all these administrations had to be be rebuilt after World War II and that the then existing regimes on the various levels put their mark on them. Moreover, as has already been explained, the tradition of the high civil service has tended to be on the conservative side, which has an impact on existing party affiliations. But again there have been few complaints that such membership has led to partisanship in the treatment of the public. There is also good reason to believe that as the older civil servants pass towards retirement, their successors may show a more balanced distribution as far as party affiliation is concerned.

It is possible to argue that in democratic regimes which have been stable and established for a long time, the poor quality of civil servants is always regrettable and wasteful, but does not necessarily constitute a danger to the regime. In fact, one might even suspect that the stability of institutions could be measured (though one might wish that it were not) by the degree to which they can be managed by mediocre men. But when a regime is of more recent origin, then the substandard level of its servants might reflect not merely on the service but also on the regime itself, and thus endanger it. In this case the words of the Swiss jurist, Fritz Fleiner, may be applied, ". . . one can govern more or less with bad laws if one has good officials, but if you have bad officials, even the best laws will do little good." The generally high quality of the German civil service is, therefore, a matter of great importance.

CHAPTER EIGHT

The Legislature

THE LEGISLATURE of the German Federal Republic is bicameral and is composed of the Federal Diet (*Bundestag*) and the Federal Council (*Bundesrat*). The *Bundestag* resembles other legislatures on the European continent, being popularly elected proportionate to the distribution and the will of the people. The *Bundesrat*, on the other hand, is a completely unique assembly both in its composition and in its functions. For this reason it will be discussed first.

The Federal Council (Bundesrat)

The members of the *Bundesrat* are not elected but *appointed* by the governments of the German Laender whose members they are. They are subject to instructions, may be withdrawn at any time, and must vote as a bloc from the *Land* they represent.

Each *Land* has a maximum of five and a minimum of three members in the *Bundesrat*. North Rhine-Westphalia, Bavaria, Baden-Wuertemberg, and Lower Saxony have five members each; Hesse, Rhineland-Palatinate, and Schleswig Holstein, four; while Hamburg, Bremen, and the Saar have three each. In addition, West Berlin has four nonvoting members in the *Bundesrat*. This distribution thus reflects to some degree the difference in population between the Laender, but is in no way proportionate when one considers that the most populous *Land*, North Rhine-Westphalia, has 15,852,500 inhabitants, while Bremen has only 704,300.[1]

The special nature of the *Bundesrat* has an historical origin that has also contributed to the special nature of German federal-

[1] This figure reflects the census of 1956.

118

ism. The Constitution of the German Empire of 1871 reflected Bismarck's idea that the princes of the Laender should in some way participate in the sovereignty of the Reich. The *Bundesrat* of the Reich thus became not only the more influential of the two houses of parliament, but, in a sense, also a "second government." The predominance of Prussia expressed itself by the fact that the Chairman of the Council was at one and the same time Chancellor of the Reich and Prime Minister of Prussia. In the Weimar Republic of 1919 this body, then renamed *Reichsrat*, was somewhat diminished and the predominance of Prussia was modified through a statutory split in its delegation. The chairmanship passed to a member of the Reich Cabinet and was no longer held by the head of the Prussian delegation.

The Basic Law of 1949 restored the name *Bundesrat*. Prussia having disappeared, that particular problem no longer existed. The chairmanship rotates regularly between the heads of the respective Laender governments, including that of Berlin, despite the nonvoting status of the Berlin delegation.

The power of the *Bundesrat* is significant but its influence is even greater. The Constitution provides a number of specific subjects on which the *Bundesrat* has an absolute veto, in other words, in these domains no legislation can be passed without its consent. This is the case regarding constitutional amendments for which a two-thirds majority in both houses is required, as well as for legislation concerning the Laender in administrative, fiscal, or territorial regards. These are very broad categories. Experience shows that approximately half of all bills, including the most important ones, fall into this category.

The *Bundesrat* has taken the point of view that in all matters in which *Land* administrative authorities have an administrative duty to perform, the *Bundesrat* must be co-determinant. This interpretation has been contested, but in practice the *Bundesrat* has had its way. The ratification of treaties follows the same procedure as legislation, which means that treaties concerning subjects in which the *Bundesrat* has an absolute veto can be ratified only with its express consent.

Wherever the Constitution vests power in the federal government to issue executive orders which have to be carried out by Laender organs, the consent of the Federal Council is necessary.

This is also true in those cases in which the federal government has the right of supervision or has the right to issue general guidelines (*Weisungen*). As we have already seen, the consent of the Federal Council is essential, where, in times of emergency, the federal government places the police forces of the Laender under its control, as well as in the case of legislative emergency.

In all other cases the *Bundesrat* has only a suspensive veto.

All government bills must first be introduced in the *Bundesrat*, which may comment on them before passing them on to the *Bundestag*. After the latter has passed the bill, it returns to the *Bundesrat*. If this house does not give its consent, it may demand that a conference committee be called composed of representatives of both houses. This is the only body where members of the *Bundesrat* are technically not bound by instructions, but in view of their absolute control by their Laender governments, the provision is somewhat theoretical. Where the *Bundesrat* has only a suspensive veto and where the conference committee does not succeed in settling differences between the two houses, the *Bundestag* has the opportunity to overrule the *Bundesrat* by a simple majority. If, however, the *Bundesrat* has cast its suspensive veto with a two-thirds majority of its members, it can be overridden by the *Bundestag* only if the latter also assembles a two-thirds majority.

The *Bundesrat*, furthermore, has another advantage; its members may appear in any and all of the committees of the *Bundestag* and must be heard on their request. Even more important is the fact that the heads of the Laender governments appear only in the *Bundesrat* for relatively brief periods at a time, while the daily work, especially in the vital conference committee, is carried on by experienced high civil servants of the Laender whose skill and knowledge are frequently superior to that of members of the *Bundestag*. Moreover, the federal government and the *Bundestag* frequently have a greater interest in the speedy passage of legislation than the *Bundesrat* and the latter is therefore in a somewhat better negotiating position. For all these reasons, the *Bundestag* is somewhat more inclined to give in to the reservations of the *Bundesrat*. Of course such a complex system with two partners of such different natures could not work without the skillful cooperation of the above-mentioned conference committee which is composed of 22 members, half from each chamber. So great is the skill with which this conference committee operates that it has failed to reach agreement on only about 5 percent or less of all bills which have reached it. Here again the influence of the *Bundesrat* has been on the increase, and despite the fact that the suspensive veto of the *Bundesrat* can be overridden in half of the bills, the two chambers, in practice, are very nearly co-equal.

Thus the power of the Laender, which could easily be curtailed by the control of the federal government over both the federal and the Laender bureaucracies, is more than restored to the Laender by their important role in the *Bundesrat*.

Of course, party politics also enter the picture. The national parties tend to put pressure on the *Land* governments under their control to pass their votes in the *Bundesrat* according to national party interests. For the same reason, national issues and national figures enter Laender elections in order to influence the outcome. One distinguished writer, Heidenheimer, even goes so far as to say that "the Land cabinets have at times been reduced almost to the status of the pawns of federal politics." This state of "national" involvement in Laender affairs reached its height during the debate on the recreation of a German army when the possible need of constitutional amendments—which require the consent of the *Bundesrat*—had to be considered. However, the degree to which the national parties can influence the vote cast by the Laender groups in the *Bundesrat* is severely restricted by the fact that most Laender governments are coalitions and purely partisan votes of their delegations in the *Bundesrat* could lead to a crisis in the *Land*. Hence, in recent years, the tendency of the Laender governments to cast their votes in the *Bundesrat* in an independent fashion has increased, and the national party leaders cannot count on the Laender governments which their parties dominate to vote in a manner they desire. This has been as true of *Land* governments dominated by the CDU as of those dominated by the SPD. Because of their political composition, the Laender of Schleswig-Holstein (CDU), Rhineland Palatinate (CDU), and Hesse (SPD) are more likely than the others to vote according to partisan principles, but even there this is by no means a foregone conclusion. A further variant also enters because the complex compositions of the Laender governments make it more difficult for lobbies to influence proceedings in the *Bundesrat* than is the case both in the *Bundestag* and in the government. Only where agricultural legislation is concerned is the situation more like that in the other two branches.

Perhaps one drawback in the operation of the *Bundesrat* is the fact that many of its decisions and arguments take the form of administrative rather than political rulings, and appear too technical to the broad public to be comprehensible. Hence the true importance of that house is not widely understood in Germany. This, however, has so far not diminished the *Bundesrat's* significance which, as I have shown, has actually been on the increase.

Despite its federal character, the *Bundesrat* is a part of the national government structure. The coordination of the activities of the various *Land* governments, where desirable, does not normally take place in the *Bundesrat* but rather in special meetings of the Land Prime Ministers or Ministers. Particularly notable is the Permanent Conference of the Ministers of Education which has brought some order into this otherwise largely uncoordinated field.

The Federal Diet (Bundestag)

ELECTIONS. The Weimar Republic had a rigid proportional representation system, a list system according to which a fixed number of votes entitled a political party to a seat in Parliament. Much has been written about the supposedly disastrous effects of this system which was blamed for preserving a multi-party system and resulting in unstable coalition governments. Partly under the influence of this criticism, there was much sympathy in the Parliamentary Council for the installation of the Anglo-American single member district and plurality system. However, such ideas were frustrated by the solid opposition of the Social Democrats who feared that the greater concentration of their votes in industrial areas would handicap them under such an electoral process as against Christian Democrats whose voters, especially in rural districts, were spread more thinly. In the end a rather peculiar system was established which looked like a compromise but which in reality must be characterized as a special version of the proportional representation system.

The system works as follows: each Land is assigned a certain number of seats in the *Bundestag* according to size of population. One-half of these seats are assigned to single member districts into which the Land is divided. For that latter purpose each party establishes a list of its candidates throughout the Land. The voter marks *two votes* on his single ballot sheet: one he casts for a single candidate in his district, the other he casts for a list of the party of his choice. The vote for a single candidate is called "first vote" (*Erststimme*), that which is cast for the list is called "second vote" (*Zweitstimme*). The "second vote" in effect determines the number of seats each party obtains. They are counted according to the most widespread system of proportional representation (the d'Hondt system) and in such a way as if the single member districts did not exist. At this point a *tentative* number of seats is assigned to each party.

Then the seats gained by each party in single member districts according to the "first vote" are counted and deducted from the aforementioned number of tentative seats. What remains then are the seats which each party has won from the "Land list." The names of these candidates are simply taken from the top of each list down in the sequence indicated by the party presenting the list. The *final* number of seats thus obtained by each party is composed of (1) those won in single member districts, plus (2) those taken from the list. The total is normally that which the first preliminary count of the "second vote" determined as described above.

In a few cases it occurs that a party wins more seats in single member districts than it would be entitled to under the tentative count of "second votes" under proportional representation. In that case the party keeps all seats gained in direct elections with the result that a few seats have to be added to the total originally envisaged for the *Bundestag*. These so-called "overhang votes" (*Überhangmandate*) rarely exceed two or three throughout the Federal Republic.

The net result of this complicated system is that a party's strength is really determined by proportional representation and

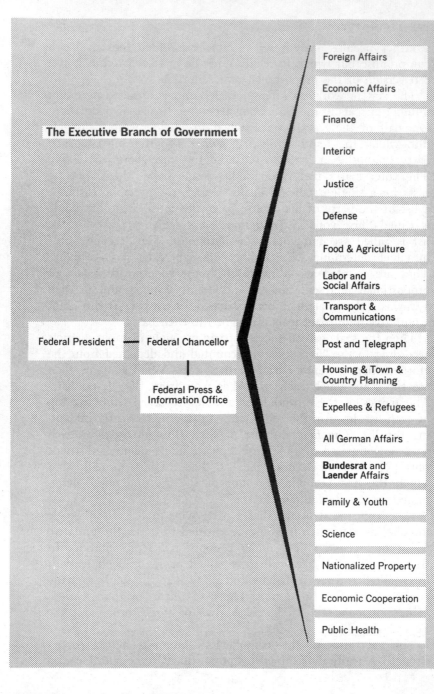

The Executive Branch of Government

Federal President — Federal Chancellor

Federal Press & Information Office

Foreign Affairs

Economic Affairs

Finance

Interior

Justice

Defense

Food & Agriculture

Labor and Social Affairs

Transport & Communications

Post and Telegraph

Housing & Town & Country Planning

Expellees & Refugees

All German Affairs

Bundesrat and **Laender** Affairs

Family & Youth

Science

Nationalized Property

Economic Cooperation

Public Health

all that the "first votes" contribute is the distribution within each party group of those directly elected and those elected on a list. Since all nominations, both for the lists and for single member districts, are made by the political parties, this split system does not really weaken the control of the party leaders over candidacies.

In one respect, however, this split system has a limited significance. The direct election of a deputy in a single member district adds to his prestige and relative independence within the party. In turn this result can be achieved only by candidates who have a sizeable local backing both within the local party organization and the population at large. That is why many candidates whose names appear on the party lists hope, some day, to be chosen for candidacy in single member districts. To be eligible, they will find it useful and necessary to pay attention to local problems and to their local personal positions. While some critics do not like this feature on grounds of "localism," it is undeniable that these realities tend to bring deputies and their voters closer together than is normally the case in countries where an undiluted system of proportional representation exists.[1]

The 22 nonvoting members from Berlin are elected by the Berlin Legislature rather than by popular vote. This difference underlines both the ambiguity of Berlin's legal position and the anxiety of the Western powers and of Germany not to provoke the Russians unnecessarily.

Because the German electoral system is essentially one of proportional representation, it has served to disprove the universal validity of at least one theory according to which the proportional election system encourages and perpetuates a multi-party system. The experience of the Federal Republic shows that the unmistakable development from a multipartite to a two-party system has not been significantly retarded by the proportional system. It was undoubtedly aided by the provision that a political party must obtain at least 5 percent of all the votes cast throughout

---

[1] Candidates may run for election in single member districts and at the same time have their names on their party's *Land* list. If elected in their single member district their names are skipped when those elected from the lists are determined. However, nobody may have his name on more than one list.

the Federal Republic or obtain at least three directly elected seats in order to obtain any seats at all. This provision was designed to discourage frivolous candidacies and also to push steadily declining parties into oblivion. This has certainly speeded up the process but cannot in itself be held responsible for the increasing tendencies towards a two-party system.

Voters are automatically registered by the authorities—a common European practice—and voting participation is generally in the high eighties. There is no equivalent to the American or British Corrupt Practices Act, but campaign expenses have been much lower than in America, though much higher than in Great Britain. The "Americanization" of election techniques—often copied from American examples, has tended to increase costs. This has worried the parties but so far no remedies have been found.

ORGANIZATION. Bonn shares the distinction of Canberra in Australia and Brasilia in Brazil in that its character as a capital city had to be artificially created although, in contrast to the aforementioned other cities, Bonn did exist as a small university town. In particular the parliament building (Bundeshaus) had to be designed and built specifically for the occasion. Only the old and gutted Reichstag building in Berlin served as a model to a limited extent. The hall of the Bundestag is large, square, and almost severely modern. Its only ornament is a rather stylized replica of the "Federal Eagle" on the wall facing the deputies. In front of it is a large podium taking up almost the entire width of the wall. In its center, in a place of particular elevation, is the large desk of the Bundestag's presiding officer and in front of that, in a lower position but still well above the floor, is the speakers' rostrum. As one faces the president's desk, there is another long rostrum to his left and a similar section to his right. On the left sit the government and the members of the cabinet, whether members of the Bundestag or not, with the Chancellor having the corner seat closest to the President's desk and the speaker's rostrum. The same elevated section to the right is reserved for members of the Bundesrat. This room has none of the intimacy of the British House of Commons and, in contrast to the French Parliament, the members of the government do not occupy the front seats but, as already described, face the house from their particular position emphasizing, so to speak, both confrontation and remoteness. Professor Grosser criticizes the absence of corridors, the "couloirs" of the French National Assembly, and the absence of places where the deputies can easily and informally meet and chat. However, the style of German parliamentary life is such that it is doubtful that merely physical or architectural changes would make a great deal of difference.

The speaker, called president, is elected by secret ballot and has extensive powers. German practice regards him as something of the "householder" and vests in him supervision over the housekeeping functions of the *Bundestag*. He also has considerable disciplinary powers, having the right to exclude a deputy for as much as thirty days. He is also something like a Chief of Police (*Polizeigewalt*) for the premises which have their own security personnel and from which normally the police of the *Land* North Rhine-Westphalia and of the city of Bonn are excluded. However, the president of the *Bundestag* may call on those local police forces should it become necessary. In contrast to the Weimar period, the *Bundestag* has seen relatively little commotion, and its proceedings are generally calm and sometimes dull. Thus far the *Bundestag* has had two presiding officers, the late Hermann Ehlers, and Eugen Gerstenmaier. Both have conducted their office with firmness and dignity, and both, members of the CDU, have been leading Protestants.

The presiding officer is assisted by the Council of Elders (*Ältestenrat*) composed of deputies of all parties represented in the *Bundestag* and selected on the basis of age, not seniority. The Council of Elders has some of the functions of a steering committee. It is responsible for producing agreement concerning distribution of the work load and it selects the committee chairmanships, some of which go to members of the opposition.

The *Bundestag* may refuse to seat a member if his election was illegal or if he carried some other impediments recognized by law. However, the persons thus excluded may appeal to the Federal Constitutional Court for a final ruling.

Members of the *Bundestag* have the customary immunities of European parliaments but these have been spelled out in greater detail in the German Constitution than elsewhere and there are certain innovations. Article 46 prescribes that no deputy may be "prosecuted in the courts or subjected to disciplinary action or otherwise called to account outside the *Bundestag* because of a vote passed or an utterance made by him in the *Bundestag* or in one of its committees." An exception is made in the case of "defamatory libel" which is precisely defined in the German penal code and is designed to prevent the misuse of parliamentary immunity as often happened in the Weimar Republic.[2] However, even in that case, the *Bundestag* itself would have to approve by majority vote that the deputy involved should stand trial and that is also true in all other cases of prosecution against a deputy for acts committed outside parliament.

Unusual is also the provision of Article 47 that facts and documents which a deputy may acquire in the exercise of his duties are "privileged communications" which he may not be obliged to divulge. Nor may these documents be seized. A deputy may divest himself of that right but the *Bundestag* itself cannot oblige him to do so.

Members of the *Bundestag* receive compensations which are figured out in a rather complicated fashion. They receive, first of all, a "compensation" (*Aufwandtsentschädigung*) of 22.5 percent of a cabinet minister's salary. Secondly they receive a per diem which is rounded out to DM 500 (about $130) per month. But curiously penalties are also assessed against them for non-attendance. For failing to sign the register on days of sessions, DM 30 (about $7.80), or for missing plenary sessions DM 50 (about $12.50), are deducted for each such day. Missing a roll call vote costs them DM 25 (about $6.20). But these penalties can be avoided by requesting and receiving official leave from the presiding officer, normally a routine request. Members also receive an allowance of DM 600 per month (about $150) for office expenses including secretarial help, as well as a travel allowance depending on the distance between their residence and Bonn. They also enjoy free train travel and franking privileges.

These allowances are far from adequate, and although the

[2] German Penal Code (St. G. B.) Article 187 defines defamatory libel (*verleumderische Beleidigung*) as the assertion of a fact which is capable of making a person appear contemptible or degraded in public opinion if that assertion is proved to be untrue, and if its untruthfulness was known to the accused.

members of the German parliament are certainly better off than their British colleagues, they lag far behind the financial situation of their American colleagues. While no reliable figures on the social background of *Bundestag* deputies are available, educational statistics give a clue. In the fourth *Bundestag* (1961–1965), 58 percent had higher education (university or technical colleges). Leading were lawyers (113 deputies out of 521).

Any political party whose deputies in the *Bundestag* number at least 15 has the right to organize a formal parliamentary group called *Fraktion*. This is in fact the organized party caucus, and only those parties having *Fraktionen* are entitled to have their members in the various committees of the *Bundestag* including the Council of Elders. It is in these party caucuses, *Fraktionen*, that a major portion of parliamentary work is accomplished and it is therefore necessary to understand their functions.

Article 38, section 1, of the Basic Law provides that deputies are "representatives of the whole nation" and that they are "not bound by orders and instructions and are subject only to their conscience." This provision is both unrealistic and misleading. It was designed to abolish the binding force of caucus decisions, called *Franktionszwang*, which was typical of the Weimar Republic. But clearly political realities are stronger than legal provisions especially since the Weimar Constitution had a similar article, while at the same time upholding *Franktionszwang* officially. Perhaps it would be more correct to say that this constitutional provision was designed to demonstrate the growth of democratic institutions in contradistinction to the Laender constitutions of the early 19th Century in which guilds and aristocratic groups gave their deputies directions. Today, however, the situation is quite different and it would be wholly impractical to think that a deputy who can be nominated only by his party and who has absolutely no real possibility of running as an independent, could simply act only as his conscience dictates.

Still, the inner working of the *Fraktion* is not undemocratic. It is the purpose of the caucus to decide on the position which a party shall take in the full meeting of the house. *Fraktion* meetings are, therefore, confidential and the members exercise their free speech quite liberally. At the same time, the *Fraktion* decides who shall do what and distributes the various offices and positions within the *Fraktion*. It is correct, therefore, to say that the *Fraktion* decides whether a deputy remains a backbencher, to use the British term, or whether he is to be a more important member, or even whether he is to be in the front rank where he would be a candidate for a cabinet position if his party enters the government. The conduct of the individual deputy is consequently quite likely to be governed by these realities. Complete independence is possible only for a deputy who does not wish to be renominated and who has a spot in private life to which he can return. It is not possible for those with political ambitions or those who are dependent on their seat in the legislature for their livelihood. Even those deputies who are relatively independent of their party leadership because they have strong professional organizations, lobbies, labor unions, etc., behind them, cannot carry their independence too far, because their "clients" expect them to play an effective role in parliament which in turn means that they must play an effective role in the *Fraktion*. To be effective means to participate in the debate, to acquire a reputation for knowledge and also for discipline. After a while a deputy may have acquired a reputation for sound knowledge and judgment although he may not be known to the public at large. Here he acquires some influence but less independence. It is only when he climbs to the top of the party and *Fraktion* ladder that he acquires not only great influence but also considerable independence because a portion of the party's reputation and effectiveness is in his hands, and he is as necessary to the party as it is to him.

Under those circumstances it is clear that the image of a parliament conducting a public debate according to which each deputy votes his conscience is totally erroneous when applied to the regular meetings of the *Bundestag*. By the time these debates take place, each *Fraktion* has established its position and distributed the roles. Now the discussion is primarily in terms of the party's public image or, if an election approaches, in electoral terms. Even heat and indignation will frequently be artificial rather than real, although the most careful stage management slips from time to time. But in the *Fraktion* and sometimes in the equally confidential committee meetings, discussion is real and can be meaningful. Beyond that, each group usually votes and speaks as a bloc and only mavericks swim against the stream. This is particularly true in the Social Democratic Party which has virtually complete discipline whereas split votes occur quite frequently in the CDU and its sister party the CSU. This is also true of what remains of the FDP. Important issues, however, are likely to find all parties unified or nearly unified around the decisions of their *Fraktionen*.

The committee structure of the *Bundestag* is similar to that of the American and French legislatures: there is a committee responsible for every important ministry, such as foreign affairs, defense, etc. Membership in the committees is confined to those parties having *Fraktionen,* and the composition and chairmanships of the committees are subject to agreement reached between the *Fraktionen.* German committees do not have the extensive staffs of their American colleagues. For that they must rely on the ministries concerned, or on specialists from the universities of Bonn and Cologne in particular because of their proximity. However the relationship between the government and the academic world is not as close in Germany as it is in the United States, and considerable expertise is available in the *Bundestag* and in the *Bundesrat* themselves on many subjects. Nonetheless, some university professors have gone into the government on a full time basis, such as Chancellor Ludwig Erhard. Others such as Under Secretary for Foreign Affairs Karl Carstens and SPD leader Carlo Schmid continue their government work while still meeting some of their classes.

Beside the regular standing committees there are also special investigating committees. Article 44 of the Constitution entitles the *Bundestag* to organize such committees at any time. They are empowered to hold hearings and investigations on their own authority. It is mandatory for them to act when one-fourth of the committee's members demand it. In contrast to the American theory on the subject, these committees can hold their hearings and draw their conclusions regardless of any bearing they may have on legislation past, present, or future. The purpose is primarily to throw the spotlight of public attention on situations which may require it.

Traditionally most investigations have concerned (1) economic and social questions capable of leading to legislation or legislative changes; (2) alleged mismanagement or misconduct in the administration; (3) contested elections; and (4) unusual criminal cases and instances of corruption of major public interest. The investigating committees have quasi-judicial status and have the right to compel the giving of evidence, but they may not themselves order arrests or conduct searches. The Constitution prescribes that the rules of criminal procedure are to be applied analagously to the procedure of investigating committees, but the nature of their work is sufficiently different from that of courts as to make this analogy applicable in only a restricted number of cases. In practice no separate investigating committees are set up, but 141 existing committees are reconstituted as investigating committees. Thus, for instance, the Defense Committee investigated corrupt practices in the procurement of uniforms.

In addition to the already-mentioned Council of Elders, there is also the so-called "Permanent Committee" (*Ständiger Ausschuss*). While all other committees meet only when the *Bundestag* itself is in session, the Permanent Committee is not confined to those periods. Its main task, in fact, is to exercise the right of parliamentary supervision over the Executive when the *Bundestag* is not in session, especially between the dissolution of one legislature and the convocation of its successor. The Permanent Committee has the same rights as all other committees including that of conducting investigations. In fact, it may be compared to a small version of the entire house itself. However, it does not have the right to pass a vote of nonconfidence.

A rather peculiar position has been created by a constitutional amendment enacted March 19, 1956 (Art. 45b) under which the *Bundestag* elects a Defense Commissioner (*Wehrbeauftragter*) "to safeguard the basic rights and to assist the *Bundestag* in exercising parliamentary control." The authors of this amendment clearly had in mind the Weimar period during which the army occupied the position of "state within the state." The new concept of "the citizen soldier" made it desirable that the discipline and the civic organization within the army should be in line with requirements of a democracy. The Defense Commissioner was, therefore, to be an independent agent of the *Bundestag* without any obligations to either the Ministry of Defense or the military establishment itself, and to report grievances and shortcomings to the *Bundestag*, in particular to its Committee on Defense.

The effectiveness of this institution has been somewhat beclouded by the controversies involving former Admiral Hellmuth Heye who resigned in 1964. What became controversial was not so much Admiral Heye's vigor in ferreting out undue hardships in training procedures and other shortcomings, but rather that the Admiral thought it necessary to attract attention to his findings by publishing them in a mass circulation illustrated weekly.

There is no doubt that civilian and parliamentary supervision over the German army is a matter of the greatest importance in view of Germany's recent past. However, malpractices and overly severe discipline are only some of the problems of an extremely complex situation. The men who reshaped the German army were extremely conscious of their task, which was not to recreate the old Prussian system but to establish an army of citizen soldiers.

However, the very close integration of the German army into NATO and the particularly intimate relationship between the United States and German armies, have contributed to a generally favorable development despite the discovery of shortcomings and some instances of excessive severity on the part of training officers and noncommissioned officers. While the public attention is frequently attracted to instances of survival of "Prussian" drill practices, a more severe long-range problem arises from the very fact that the formerly overbearing status of the armed forces has been diminished in line with democratic practices and there are severe shortages in both commissioned and noncommissioned officers' ranks.

Civilian superiority over the army has been firmly established by the Federal Republic's first Defense Minister, Theodor Blank, and in particular by his two successors, Franz Josef Strauss and Kai Uwe von Hassel. Moreover, the Defense Committee of the *Bundestag* has proven itself very effective in supervising the armed forces. (Military offences, such as excessively harsh training methods leading to the death or injury of soldiers, are tried before regular civilian [criminal] courts, not by courts martial.) In part this was made possible by the close cooperation between the CDU/CSU chairmen and the SPD deputy chairmen of the committee. It would seem likely that even if the position of the Defense Commissioner were to diminish, as appears probable at this time, parliamentary supervision over the armed forces would not necessarily be eliminated.

LEGISLATION.   Bills are introduced in the *Bundestag*: either the government (cabinet), the *Bundesrat,* or any member of the *Bundestag* may do so. However, a government bill must first be submitted to the *Bundesrat* which then has three weeks to give an opinion. This prior submission of a government bill to the *Bundesrat* is not wholly a part of the legislative process: it would be more correct to call it an obligatory request for an advisory opinion. At this stage the *Bundesrat* neither accepts nor rejects the bill. Similarly a bill introduced in the *Bundestag* by the *Bundesrat* must first pass through the hands of the cabinet which then submits the bill to the *Bundestag.* In doing so, the cabinet gives its views about the bill. However, neither that bill's submission to the *Bundestag* nor the advisory opinion of the cabinet are optional (Article 77).

Once introduced, the bill is subjected to a process called "first reading" which is a discussion on the general principles of the bill and not on its details. Amendments are not considered at this stage. If a bill successfully passes this "first reading," it is then referred to committee, sometimes to several committees. After having been reported out by the committee, a bill is then subjected to a "second reading," which goes into more detail, especially toward the end of that stage when amendments are considered for the first time. Only international treaties must be discussed and decided (ratified) without amendment. A "third reading" finally goes into the finer details of a bill, and amendments are taken up if seconded by at least ten members. A vote ends the "third reading" and determines the fate of the bill in the *Bundestag.*

A considerable speeding up of this cumbersome procedure is possible by unanimous consent of all members of the *Bundestag* present, which allows all three readings to be rushed through in a single day. Other rules may also be streamlined upon unanimous consent. Normally, however, any member of the *Bundestag* may speak for an hour and may speak longer if permission is granted by a majority. On the other hand it is possible that the

Council of Elders may decide upon more stringent time limits.

After the bill has passed the *Bundestag*, it is now formally submitted to the *Bundesrat*. Within two weeks of its receipt, the *Bundesrat* may demand that a conference committee be called to iron out differences. If this committee comes up with a new version of the bill not previously adopted in the *Bundestag*, a single and fourth reading in the *Bundestag* is now sufficient to pass it.

As we have seen previously, the *Bundesrat* has both a suspensive and an absolute veto. In the case of a bill for which the Constitution does not specifically require the *Bundesrat*'s approval, that consent may either be given by the *Bundesrat* in a formal fashion or the *Bundesrat* may simply do nothing; in either case the bill becomes law, in the latter instance after the expiration of a two-week period from the date of submission or a one-week period after a report has been rendered by the Conference Committee. If the *Bundesrat* decides to cast its suspensive veto, it can do so only after the conference committee has met and has failed to achieve agreement. The *Bundestag* may override this suspensive veto by a simple majority. If, however, the *Bundesrat* has cast its suspensive veto *(Einspruche)* by a vote of two-thirds of its members, then the *Bundestag* has to override it also by a two-thirds vote, but only of those present, provided the vote for over-riding embraces at least one half of all members of the *Bundestag* whether present or not.

We have already seen that there are a number of important issues where the *Bundesrat* has an absolute veto and where therefore lack of consent brings the legislative effort to a halt. The system works fairly smoothly. The fourth *Bundestag* (1961–1965) received 626 bills, 108 of which were not passed.

Intriguing are the provisions regarding the ratification of international treaties. Such ratification is undertaken by an ordinary legislative act; this means in effect that if a treaty deals with a subject on which, if it were an ordinary act of legislation, the *Bundesrat* has an absolute veto, then the *Bundesrat* also has a veto over the act of ratification. Otherwise the veto is suspensive, as with analagous items of legislation.

As we have seen, the role of the *Bundesrat* is essentially constructive and its influence can be felt at all stages of the procedure and not merely in the final vote. That it is much easier for the smaller *Bundesrat* to amass a two-thirds majority than it is for the larger *Bundestag* to do so provides an additional edge of influence for the *Bundesrat* regarding the legislative subjects over which it has only a suspensive veto.

DISSOLUTION AND LEGISLATIVE EMERGENCY. The Weimar Constitution gave the government a right of virtually unlimited dissolution—with the consent of the Reich President, but the exercise of this right did not increase the stability of German governments; if anything, it had quite the contrary effect. The Constitution of 1949 by contrast comes close to eliminating that right. There remain a few cases where dissolution is theoretically possible but they are highly theoretical indeed.

We have already seen (Article 63, Section 4) that if the *Bundestag* fails to elect a Chancellor nominated by the President, and if it fails to elect another candidate within two weeks thereafter, and if a candidate emerges only with a plurality, the President has the choice either of appointing him or of dissolving the *Bundestag* within seven days.

A more probable event might occur after a Chancellor had asked the *Bundestag* for a vote of confidence and had failed to receive it. In that case, he might recommend dissolution of the *Bundestag* but,,as we have seen, the *Bundestag* might elect a new Chancellor and thus nullify its own dissolution.

Another residue of the Weimar past is the power of legislative emergency. The Weimar Constitution endowed the Executive with exceptional and notorious emergency powers in its infamous Article 48. Commentators have called it the "dictatorship article" of the Constitution. Little of this remains in the Constitution of 1949 except a curious and highly impractical provision which stipulates (Article 81) the following situation: if the federal Chancellor has (1) asked for a vote of confidence and has been refused, and if (2) the *Bundestag* has *not* elected a new Chancellor, and if (3) the *Bundestag* has refused to enact a bill which the government has declared to be "urgent," the government may, instead of urging dissolution, recommend to the federal President that he proclaim a "state of legislative emergency" (*Gesetzgebungsnotstand*). The President may issue such a proclamation, however, only (4) with the consent of the *Bundesrat*.

After the proclamation of this "state of legislative emergency," the *Bundestag* has one more chance. It may yet pass the bill which has been declared "urgent," and if it does so, the state of legislative emergency disappears. If, however, it fails to do so, and passage of an "urgent" bill in a form not acceptable to the government would be regarded as tantamount to the refusal to pass, the bill will nevertheless be "deemed enacted"—if the *Bundesrat* consents thereto. The Constitution itself may not be amended or modified in this way.

A state of legislative emergency can last only six months from the date of its proclamation. During that period other bills may also be enacted in the same manner but in each case the procedure outlined above must be repeated. It is also understood that the *Bundestag* may not repeal these laws within the six month period of the "state of legislative emergency," although it may do so later on. After the six months have passed, no second state of legislative emergency may be proclaimed during the same term of the same Chancellor.

Both the dissolution and the "legislative emergency" articles of the Constitution reflect the fears of the "fathers" of 1949 lest a multi-party system and feeble coalition regimes once again paralyze legislation and administration. One might reflect that even under such circumstances, these two remedies are of doubtful effectiveness. As far as dissolution is concerned, experience shows that one of the evils of a multi-party system is the fact that each party has a large enough clientele to guarantee its survival, and hence repeated elections do not generally create more viable political conditions nor more stable majorities. As for the "state of legislative emergency," the procedure is so cumbersome that there is real doubt that it could ever be applied. At any rate, the need for a consent by the *Bundesrat* does constitute an important safeguard which the Weimar Constitution did not have.

In reality it is German political development which has decided this question. The political trend has gone towards simplification rather than greater complexity of the party system and beside the two large political giants, the CDU/CSU and the SPD, only one other party, the FDP, has managed to remain alive in the *Bundestag*. Hence the need for either of the aforementioned measures seems remote. Moreover the deputies have not forgotten the lessons of Weimar and it appears most unlikely that they would bring about again the periodic legislative paralysis which characterized the 1900 to 1933 period. The complete absence of extremist parties in the *Bundestag* renders this assumption an even safer one.

LEGISLATIVE REALITIES AND EXECUTIVE-LEGISLATIVE RELATIONSHIPS. The constitutional system of the German Federal Republic makes it possible to see more power in the hands of parliament than there actually is. True, parliament appears to have the final say on legislative decisions. Yet, in effect, the German parliament participates less in the formation of policy than is the case in several other countries. In part this is due to the absence of independent staffs at the disposal of the *Bundestag* and its committees, and its resultant dependence on the staffs of the ministries. Although, as we have said, there is expertise available among the members of parliament and especially of the *Bundesrat*, laws these days cover so many technical subjects and are so numerous that detailed examination becomes very difficult for private members of the house. The various special interest groups and lobbies have understood this, and their relations and contacts therefore have been established to the ministries and party executives rather than to the deputies. Moreover, a ministry will deal only with national organizations, and this too has contributed to the centralization and power of those groups. The lobbies deal primarily with civil servants and their political superiors, rarely with deputies.

Most of the work of the *Bundestag* takes place in committee meetings which are not open to the public. This does not mean the same as being secret; a special decision has to be made to subject a committee meeting to the cover of secrecy. But the discussions are not public in order to permit considerable freedom of speech, which at times may not coincide with party dicta, and also to permit the participation on an informal basis of numerous experts from the ministries and sometimes from professional organizations, chambers, unions, and other interest groups. In general it can be said that the work of the committees is quite thorough and that the reports which reach the floor of the house are often characterized by a high level of performance.

It is also in the committees where the debate between or the cooperation between ministers and leaders of the opposition can take place when there is mutual readiness for it.

But the control of parliament over the government and the government's control over parliament emerges from the political rather than the constitutional or legislative reality. As long as there is a solid majority behind the government, the willingness of that majority to become very critical of its own government will naturally be modified by the knowledge that if it goes too far, the party may be in trouble at the next election. Even the opposition finds it sometimes preferable to acquire a high measure of influence over governmental decisions by being reasonable and cooperative or by placing some of its adherents in high ministerial positions than by a constant confrontation. As we have seen, it has been particularly important for the leaders of the Social Democratic opposition not to acquire the reputation of being negative obstructionists.

This has not been always easy for the opposition because the German public tends to undervalue the role of the opposition in a democracy and to focus its attention on government policy. That the opposition has nevertheless been a positive and constructive one speaks well for the leadership of the Social Democratic Party as well as for the evolution of the German parliamentary system.

The opposition and also some dissident elements in the government party have opportunities to put the government on the spot by directing formal questions at the government. They may be "small" (*Kleine Anfrage*) or "large" (*Grosse Anfrage*) inquiries. They require 15 or 30 signatures respectively. While the "small" inquiry is usually answered in writing, an oral answer is customary to the "large" inquiry, plus a subsequent debate which makes the procedure something akin to the interpellation of the French Third and Fourth Republics. These inquiries, however, are not always a tool of the opposition; the government itself may fabricate an occasion to give itself an opportunity to open a debate on questions that it wishes to bring before the public. However, twice as many "large" inquiries are launched by the opposition as by the government parties.

A new system was instituted in February, 1965. Called the

"Current Events Hour" *(Aktuelle Stunde)*, this debate is limited to one hour not counting statements of Cabinet members. Each speaker is limited to five minutes, and no statements must be read. Cabinet members have promised also to adhere to the five-minute rule. This procedure is designed to make possible quick discussion of topics of immediate significance and time-liness.

Because the government is not likely to be in serious trouble in the parliament as long as it controls a majority, it is the more subtle form of the debate and the inquiry, rather than the vote of confidence, through which parliament may exercise a certain measure of control. The government in turn exercises a large, and in fact far larger, measure of control through the imposition of its party discipline and the knowledge on the part of the deputies that if they go too far they may bring their own gov-ernment and therefore their own party into difficulties. This discipline has been near perfect among Social Democrats but has never been complete among the Christian Democrats even dur-ing the days of Chancellor Adenauer's greatest power. It has been less than perfect under Chancellor Erhard and it does not control the CDU's sister party, the Christian Social Union, which has its own leadership although it shares one *Fraktion* with the CDU. But if the CSU in particular has been able at times to be quite outspoken in opposition to the government, this has been only insofar as there was no danger of bringing the govern-ment down.

For all these reasons, the liaison between the government and the chief of its *Fraktion* is of special importance, and the leader of the parliamentary group *(Fraktionsvorsitzender)* exercises con-siderable influence and power. After 1961 this role was filled with great dignity and effectiveness by the former Foreign Minister, Dr. Heinrich von Brentano. Especially in the several crises involv-ing Adenauer's leadership, Brentano proved a man of great cir-cumspection and prestige who deserves much credit for having kept his party together in difficult moments. After Brentano's death in 1964, his place was taken by a young but rising former minister, Dr. Rainer Barzel. The fact that Barzel refused another cabinet post in the Erhard government in order to become Acting Chairman and then Chairman of the CDU group shows the great importance of that office. On the opposition side, the party's longtime leader, Erich Ollenhauer, and after his death the very gifted Deputy Chairman, Fritz Erler, filled that office with great distinction.

It is certainly possible to criticize this or that feature of the German parliamentary system. But it must not be forgotten that one of the main reasons for the failure of the Weimar Regime was its inability to develop governmental leadership and a relationship of cooperation with the parliament. On both these counts the government of Bonn has been a great advance over its Weimar predecessor. That much of the credit belongs to the Federal Republic's first Chancellor, Dr. Konrad Adenauer, whose austere and imperious personality dominated the formative years of the new Germany, can hardly be doubted. Yet the constructive and restrained attitude of the opposition should also not be overlooked. Since the Chancellorship passed from Adenauer to Erhard, the domination of the scene by the Chancellor has been lessened. Nevertheless the system has not been shaken to its foundation, and in that alone lies considerable evidence that the system works.

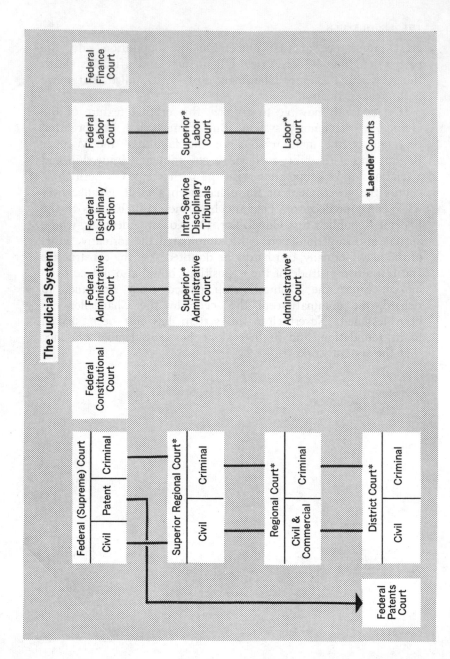

The Judicial System

Federal (Supreme) Court
- Civil
- Patent
- Criminal

Federal Constitutional Court

Federal Administrative Court

Federal Disciplinary Section

Federal Labor Court

Federal Finance Court

Superior Regional Court*
- Civil
- Criminal

Superior* Administrative Court

Intra-Service Disciplinary Tribunals

Superior* Labor Court

Regional Court*
- Civil & Commercial
- Criminal

Administrative* Court

Labor* Court

District Court*
- Civil
- Criminal

Federal Patents Court

*Laender Courts

CHAPTER NINE

The Judiciary

A NUMBER of writers have pointed to a certain rigidity in the German attitude towards the function of law.[1] Detailed codes and procedures are designed to define practically all problems in sight, and to prescribe remedies. While the Anglo-American legal tradition looks upon law as one way by which a compromise can be achieved between conflicting social claims, the German legal tradition is inclined to look upon law as the apex of all values and wisdom. Hence legalistic conformity to texts rather than practical social solutions has played a major role in public debates. As a result, codes of great brilliance and incisiveness have been developed in Germany, and lawyers as well as judges have been thoroughly trained in their use. As Professor Heidenheimer says:

Implicit is the premise that the written law is self-sufficient and that the codes, together with the statutes through which they are implemented and amended, constitute a key capable of deciding all problems that come before the courts.

This attitude has produced not only the positivism which Professor Heidenheimer underscores but also a certain neutrality towards social values and political realities. The "neutrality" even towards democracy which characterized the civil service in the Weimar Republic was particularly noticeable among judges and permitted them to serve divers masters without suffering great upsets. Naturally there were exceptions, but the courts by and large offered the least resistance to the take-over by the Nazis. This does not mean that most of the German judges or lawyers were Nazis or that they are now. It does mean, however, that

---

[1] Especially Herbert Spiro, *Government by Constitution*, New York: Random House, 1958.

the philosophy which permitted judges to be untroubled by the immoral use of the law as long as the rules were correctly enacted by the law-giver, does not commend itself as a cornerstone of the democratic system.

In view of these antecedents, it is perhaps somewhat surprising that the Constitution of 1949 greatly extended the power of the judiciary; so much so, in fact, that some writers have used the term "judiciary state." In part this is probably due to the influence of the American model which impressed the Parliamentary Council perhaps all the more as it was uncertain about the degree to which Germany's future parliamentary institutions would stand up under the strain.

The basic attitude of German judges is difficult to change because, like their French and Italian colleagues, they are not selected from the Bar but spend their entire legal life at the law schools of the universities and at court. They thus lack the balancing experience of having at one time or another represented clients and defendants as well as plaintiffs and the state. In the long run their attitude can be modified by a greater open-mindedness to social phenomena and realities, especially in the appraisal of the functions of government. But for the time being the record of the regular German judiciary is not inspiring in every respect, and there have been a number of decisions by inferior courts, dealing with Nazi criminals as well as with those who rebelled against them, in which the record has been mixed, to say the least.

It should be noted, however, that the German government as well as the governments of the Laender have been quite mindful of these events and have tried to remedy them. Also the newspapers and the public have reacted unfavorably to overly formalistic judges.

Perhaps one particularly dramatic event in which conflict between formal jurisprudence and the validity of broader principles and social realities was illustrated was in 1964 and 1965 when the statute of limitations would have made it impossible to try still-undiscovered cases of war crimes.[2] The government

---

[2] In contrast to many countries like the United States (except for one state) Germany has a twenty-year statute of limitation for homicide. However, any formal indictment even against a fugitive interrupts the statute

and the parliament realized the undesirability of letting such criminals escape and yet were hesitant to grant an exception from the general rule, partly because of the former misuse by the Nazis of "exceptional" rules and laws. In the end the *Bundestag* voted, on March 25, 1965, to extend the statute of limitations for war crimes and Nazi atrocities for another five years, that is, until January 1, 1970. The vote was overwhelming, 344 to 96, with most CDU/CSU and all SPD votes in favor, while the FDP was opposed. This decision was taken largely in response to world opinion, while public opinion polls in Germany had revealed a sizable majority of Germans opposed to the extension, presumably because they did not want the past constantly stirred up. The Minister of Justice, Ewald Bucher, resigned in protest, holding the extension law to be unconstitutional. An eventual court test would, therefore, seem likely.

THE ORDINARY COURTS SYSTEM. Only the top courts of the three judicial pyramids, Ordinary, Administrative, and Constitutional, are federal courts. The lower echelons, inasmuch as they exist, are courts of the Laender and apply both federal and *Land* legislation.

There is no German equivalent to the American or British justice of the peace. The lowest step of the court hierarchy is a regular court known as *Amtsgericht*, which we shall translate as district court.[3] District courts are found in every significant town. Sometimes a single judge takes care of all business; sometimes, in larger centers, several judges officiate, each one specializing in different categories of cases. This type of court has jurisdiction in litigation involving sums under German marks (DM) 1,000 (about $250) as well as probate and similar cases. In criminal cases (other than minor infractions) the trial court is composed of one professional judge and two lay judges *(Schöffen)*.

The next higher court, the regional court *(Landgericht*, in

---

of limitation. For instance, if such a top Nazi leader as Martin Bormann were found to be still alive and could be brought to Germany, he could still be tried if an indictment was found against him within the period covered by the statute of limitations.

[3] There is no proper translation for the term *Amtsgericht* or *Landgericht* as neither are descriptive. We have chosen "District Court" for *Amtsgericht* and "Regional Court" for *Landgericht*. Note, the judicial district of a *Landgericht* covers only a small part of a *Land*.

Berlin, *Kammergericht*), is both a court of first instance for more important matters and a court of appeals for cases decided by the district court. When engaged in civil cases, either on appeal or in original jurisdiction (with unlimited amounts), the court is composed of three regular judges. In criminal cases the court's composition is more complicated. If it is concerned with minor offenses on appeal from a single judge's verdict in the district court, it is composed of one regular judge and two lay judges. If concerned with an appeal case from a district court where a judge and two lay judges had decided, the regional court will be composed of three regular judges and two lay judges. The same composition prevails when the regional courts hold trial for a more important offense (but not a capital crime) in original jurisdiction. When hearing a case of grave offense or capital crime in original jurisdiction, the court *(Schwurgericht)* is composed of three professional judges and seven lay judges *(Geschworene)*. Despite the difference in name, the smaller group of lay judges *(Schöffen)* and the larger group *(Geschworene)* have the same functions. They are selected by lot from a list of suitable citizens maintained by the respective city councils.

In contrast to Anglo-American jurymen, the German lay judges deal with questions of both law and fact and deliberate together with the professional judges. A majority suffices. However, experience shows that the professional judges generally overshadow the lay judges.

Questionable as the lay judge system may seem, it has considerable value and merit in the commercial chambers *(Kammern für Handelssachen)* of the regional courts in which the lay judges are men of commerce and business who are chosen for their expert knowledge.

The next higher court, the superior regional court *(Oberlandesgericht)* is solely an appeals court and ordinarily has no original jurisdiction. It is also the highest ordinary court of the Laender except in Bavaria, which has a special *Land* supreme court *(Oberstes Landesgericht)*. The *Oberlandesgericht* is composed of a criminal and a civil section, called senates, each made up of three judges. It is the court of final resort for cases which had originally been heard by the district courts. For cases which originated in the regional courts, it is a court of second instance.

It does not retry a case, but either confirms the verdict of the inferior court or sends the case back for re-hearing.

The apex of the ordinary court structure is the (Supreme) Federal Court *(Bundesgerichtshof)* which resides in Karlsruhe. Its composition is curious because its judges are chosen by an election committee composed of an equal number of people appointed by the Laender ministers of justice and elected by the *Bundestag*. In civil cases it has only appellate jurisdiction for all cases originating in the regional courts. In its criminal section, the (Supreme) Federal Court has jurisdiction over cases which originated in the regional courts, but in those capital and other grave cases which were originally tried by the enlarged court of three judges and seven lay judges *(Schwurgericht)*, the case goes up on appeal directly from the regional court to the (Supreme) Federal Court without first being reviewed by the superior regional court.

Strangely enough the (Supreme) Federal Court has original jurisdiction in the case of treason which in German law not only comprises acts which aid a foreign power but also includes offenses against the internal constitutional order of the state.

In addition to its purpose as a top appellate court, the (Supreme) Federal Court is also charged with the unification of law through its jurisdiction. This is a vital task, because the period between 1945 and 1950 saw the courts of each Land go their own way and create great legal confusion which is still not quite overcome.

THE ADMINISTRATIVE COURTS. Germany's administrative court system follows closely the French pattern from which it was originally adopted. Except for a supreme financial court, neither the German Empire nor the Weimar Republic succeeded in establishing a supreme administrative court on the model of the Council of the State in France. The Nazi regime did attempt to create such a court in 1941 but war conditions and the collapse of the regime nullified this step.

Under the present constitutional system, administrative courts *(Verwaltungsgerichte)* were first re-established in the Laender and, for a court of appeals, a superior administrative court *(Oberverwaltungsgericht)* was organized in each one of them. In 1950 there was established a federal finance court *(Bundes-*

finanzgerichtshof) with its seat in Munich, and in 1952 the federal administrative court *(Bundesverwaltungsgericht)* was finally established in West Berlin.

Administrative courts deal with controversies over rights which have been allegedly damaged by an act of public authority. However, claims resulting from the state's liability for its agents go before ordinary courts and so do the salary claims of civil servants. Administrative courts also very frequently settle jurisdictional disputes between different public authorities. Their impact is not as great as that of the French Council of State but nevertheless the German administrative courts can claim solid achievements in protecting individuals against administrative arbitrariness. Civil rights cases, however, fall within the purview of the federal constitutional court.

To permit appeals from intra-service disciplinary tribunals, there has been established a Federal Disciplinary Section *(Bundesdisziplinarhof)* at the Federal Administrative Court.

LABOR COURTS AND OTHER SPECIALIZED COURTS. Special courts for labor questions are known in many European countries. A good system already existed in Germany under the Weimar Republic. It was abolished by the Nazi regime. With the re-establishment of the free trade union system it was again organized in the different Laender, all of which have labor courts and superior labor courts. In 1953 a federal supreme court for labor affairs *(Bundesarbeitsgericht)* was established in Kassel and a federal social security court *(Bundessozialgericht)* was established in the same city.

Labor courts are composed of judges representing both management and trade unions. They deal with disputes arising out of collective bargaining agreements or the failure to arrive at such agreements; disputes concerning working conditions, health, and safety; and disputes arising out of agreements between management and shop steward committees as well as out of the so-called "right of codetermination" *(Mitbestimmungsrecht)* which gives labor a part in management.

Two rather specialized courts are the Federal Finance Court *(Bundesfinanzhof)* and the (Federal) Patent Court (*[Bundes]* *Patentgericht),* both in Munich. The former includes some of the functions of the American Federal Accounting Office and hears appeals from the Land finance courts on fiscal and customs cases. By contrast, the (Federal) Patents Court in Munich is unique in that it is a federal court of first instance in patent cases. Appeals from its findings are heard by the Patents Section *(Patentsenat)* of the (Supreme) Federal Court.

THE FEDERAL CONSTITUTIONAL COURT. The summit of the entire German judicial system is a court which constitutes an innovation in German history. This is the Federal Constitutional Court *(Bundesverfassungsgericht)* whose seat is in Karlsruhe.

Because constitutional jurisdiction cannot be wholly separated from public and political affairs, this court's composition markedly differs from those of other tribunals. It is composed of two sections called senates, which divide different categories of cases between them. They are equal and independent of one another, and constitute thus a twin court. The judges are elected to the first or second senate and do not change. Each senate is composed of twelve judges, one-third of whom are judges of the highest courts ([Supreme] Federal Court, Federal Administrative Court, Federal Finance Court, etc.). They are elected for life. The other two-thirds of the judges are elected for eight years in such a way that half of them are elected every four years. Half of all the judges in all categories are elected by the *Bundestag*, and the other half by the *Bundesrat*. The former elects them indirectly through an electoral college of twelve members who in turn elect the judges by a three-fourths majority: the *Bundesrat* elects them directly by a two-thirds majority.

The purpose of this complicated system as well as the large majority required was to assure that there should be no political domination but a necessity for compromise. In actual practice the rule led to a great deal of haggling and quite unduly delayed the establishment of the court. It also resulted in one of the senates being called the "black" (Catholic) senate, and the other the "red" (Socialist) senate. The implications, however, quickly proved unfounded. All judges, whether lifetime or eight-year judges, must be fully trained jurists.

The jurisdiction of the Federal Constitutional Court is very considerable and extends to five groups of cases:

1. Most important is the right of judicial review. The Federal Constitutional Court decides whether a federal or a *Land* law is

compatible with the federal Constitution or whether *Land* law is compatible with federal law. To bring action in such cases, the Constitution requires a motion of the federal government or of a Land government or of one-third of the members of the *Bundestag.* Far more frequently, however, another procedure is followed. In a case pending before some other court, the question of the constitutionality of a law may be invoked by one of the parties. When that happens, the court must suspend proceedings and refer the question of constitutionality to the Federal Constitutional Court for its decision, which is then binding on the original court. The same is true when a question is raised as to whether a rule of the international law is part of the law of the Land and creates rights and duties for individuals. If the constitutional court of a Land intends to interpret the federal Constitution in a manner inconsistent with the past decision of the Federal Constitutional Court or of the constitutional court of another Land, it must apply for a decision to the Federal Constitutional Court.

2. The law on the Federal Constitutional Court *(Bundesverfassungsgerichtsgesetz)* of March 12, 1951, extends the jurisdiction of the Court to the so-called "Constitutional Plaint" *(Verfassungsbeschwerde).* According to Article 90 of that law, an individual who feels deprived of a civil right granted to him by the Constitution may carry his case directly to the Federal Constitutional Court. Normally this is possible only after all other remedies have been exhausted, but exceptions are possible in case of irreparable damage. By far the greatest number of cases before the Federal Constitutional Court fall into this category. The "Plaint" may be directed against any executive, legislative, or judicial act, but it can be raised only if the plaintiff's rights have been directly injured. A mere "taxpayer's suit" is not permissible.

3. The Federal Constitutional Court is responsible for the interpretation of the Constitution regarding disputes between the highest federal organs concerning their respective rights and duties. Obviously the Court does not decide all such disputes, most of which are political or administrative, but only those in which the interpretation of the Constitution is involved.

4. It decides controversies over the rights and duties of the federation and the Laender and their mutual relationships, espe-

cially with regard to the execution of federal law by Laender administrations and the federal supervision thereof.

5. It also has jurisdiction in other federation-Laender and inter-Laender controversies in public law and may decide public law disputes even within a Land if that Land does not have an appropriate judicial authority of its own. The latter is the case in only one Land today.

Finally the Constitution assigns to the Federal Constitutional Court a number of specific functions, most of which go beyond the scope of the courts. These are: (a) decisions over the loss of fundamental rights because of their misuse (Article 18); (b) suppression of political parties because of their anti-constitutional attitude (Article 21); (c) appeal against decisions of the *Bundestag* concerning the validity of an election (Article 41); (d) impeachment of the federal President (Article 61); (e) the removal of a federal judge because of offenses against the constitutional order. This can be pronounced only by the Federal Constitutional Court with a two-thirds majority and upon the demand of the *Bundestag* (Article 98, Sections 2 & 5); (f) decisions about the continued validity of older law of the former Reich (Article 126); (g) decisions of an intra-Land controversy concerning the compatibility of Land law with that Land's constitution, but only if the law of the Land specifically authorizes the Supreme Constitutional Court to render such a decision (Article 99).

Among the many important decisions of the Court, two deserve special mention here. When the Adenauer government attempted to establish a federal television network, after the Laender-controlled networks had refused to establish a second network, the Federal Constitutional Court declared this act to be unconstitutional, thereby sharply curtailing the spread of federal power. Qualified observers have duly noted the similarity between the German proposed telecommunication law and the famous American constitutional case of McCulloch versus Maryland. However, the German court wanted to protect the Laender against federal encroachment especially in the field of radio and television and possibly education, and therefore came to conclusions that differed from those of the American court.

The other important cases pertain to the prohibition of, first, the neo-Nazi Socialist Reich Party, and then the prohibition of the Communist Party. In both instances the Court found that these parties, "by reason of their aims or the behavior of their adherents seek to impair or destroy the free democratic basic order or to endanger the existence of the Federal Republic of Germany" (Article 21, Section 2), and were thus declared unconstitutional and were dissolved. In its decision against the Socialist Reich Party, the Court presented this significant definition of the "free democratic basic order" under Article 21:

An order (system) which, excluding any form of violence and arbitrariness, establishes government under the rule of law, based on the self-determination of the people according to the will of the majority at a given time and on the principles of freedom and equality. Minimal requirements of this system are: respect for the civil and human rights specified in the Basic Law, especially for the personal right to life and free development, popular sovereignty, the separation of powers, the responsibility of government, the legality of public administration, the independence of the courts, the principle of majority rule as well as the equal chances for all political parties and the right to the organisation and the activities of an opposition within the framework of the constitutional order.

These decisions were attacked on many grounds including the relationship between advocacy and public action. However, on the basis of the clear constitutional mandate, it was difficult to see how the Court could have come to different conclusions. Whether the government was politically wise in demanding the dissolution of two small and obviously declining parties is another question, but that clearly did not lie within the province of the Court. Others have questioned the desirability of having a court decide an obviously political question. However, constitutional questions are bound to be political, and as long as the Constitution specifically provides the dissolution of political parties, it would seem best that a court of the performance record of the Federal Constitutional Court should have a final check rather than that such powers be invested in a legislative or executive body.

As to the desirability of prohibiting any political party, this of course opens a rather fundamental question. It should be noted, however, that in view of Germany's recent Nazi past, the German fathers of the Constitution were particularly and understandably anxious to create some legal mechanism by which a reappearance of such movements could be nipped in the bud. Apparently this, at any rate, was achieved.

Despite its relatively recent creation, the Federal Constitutional Court has already achieved an excellent record which greatly exceeds its expectations. It has acted vigorously and courageously and has fully justified its existence. The Federal Constitutional Court, in the opinion of this writer, is one of the bright spots in the constitutional fabric of the new Germany.

CHAPTER TEN

Land and
Local Government

The Laender

THE GERMAN SYSTEM of *Land* and local government has always been basically different from that of the United States. The traditional separation existing in the United States between federal, state, and local governments constitutes a marked contrast to the fundamental unity of the German system. But this does not mean that the German Federal Republic is unitary. The German national government under the Weimar Republic, the Nazi regime, and the Federal Republic, did not ordinarily employ its own local agents but used the Land and local authorities instead. Thus, even where local government was autonomous, it always had to act as a local agent of the national authorities in addition to its autonomous functions. As a consequence, the citizen was usually confronted with only one system of bureaucracy, but local government found and still finds itself fairly tightly controlled from above. However, this control was and still is defined by detailed statutes which tend to prevent arbitrariness. Also technical efficiency played a high role on all levels of the civil service, and mayors were required to be persons of high quasi-civil service qualifications.

Under the Empire the Laender had a very great degree of autonomy, and considerable "home rule" prevailed in the municipalities. The Weimar Republic introduced a number of centralist trends and deprived the Laender of much of their autonomy. This was particularly evident in the system of taxes, all of which were collected by the national administration and then apportioned between the Reich and the Laender. In the past, apportionment among the Laender was guided neither by size nor by number of population but by the amount of income tax collected in each Land.

This type of financial administration interfered with regional and municipal planning to a large extent, for taxes were standardized and could not be adjusted to the particular needs of the community. As an experienced observer has pointed out, it was through this type of fiscal management rather than through constitutional or statutory provisions that the last vestige of German federalism became extinct. This is why the Bonn Constitution spells out in such detail an equitable distribution of fiscal powers between the federation and the Laender, in Articles 105–115, and why Article 106 was further modified in 1955 and 1956.

The great depression saddled German municipal governments with unbearable burdens. In the process of receiving additional aid from the national government, they lost more and more self-government. This provided the Nazis with a welcome opportunity to "reorganize" the entire structure of local government and to issue the uniform German Municipal Code of 1935.

After the collapse of the Nazi regime, and under Allied military government, German administrations were first established on a local level before Laender governments were reconstituted. This happened at different speeds and in different ways in the different Western zones of Germany.

As was stated in an earlier chapter, the Laender themselves were partly historical, partly artificial units. Bavaria, although it underwent some changes, mentions a one-thousand year history in its constitution, while Hesse was created out of three former units. The former Laender of Baden and Wuerttemberg, after being artificially divided into three units in order to accommodate the creation of a French zone of occupation, were finally reunited in 1952, though with difficulty and much controversy. The unified Land now bears the name Baden-Wuerttemberg. The Saarland came under French control after the Second World War, but in accordance with the treaty of June 4, 1956, it rejoined the German Federal Republic on January 1, 1957, and its special economic link to France was ended in July, 1959.

Today the German Federal Republic is composed of ten Laender: Baden-Wuerttemberg, Bavaria, Bremen, Hamburg, Hesse, Lower Saxony, North Rhine-Westphalia, Rhineland-Palatinate, Schleswig-Holstein, and the Saarland. West Berlin is in a category by itself as will be seen below.

The Laender are quite unequal in size although not nearly as much as was the case when Prussia existed. The most populated Land is North Rhine-Westphalia which includes the industrial Ruhr and Rhineland areas and at the latest census had just under 16 million inhabitants. Bavaria is the largest state in area with over 27 thousand square miles and nine and a half million inhabitants. The smallest Land in both population and area is the city-state of Bremen which has 704,000 inhabitants and covers 156 square miles only.

All Laender are organized on the principle of parliamentary democracy. They have a popularly elected legislature which, except in Bavaria, is unicameral. In most Laender the legislature is called *Landtag*, but in Hamburg and Bremen it goes by the name of *Bürgerschaft* (literally translated, Citizenry). These legislatures are elected by slightly varying forms of proportional representation and their legislative term is usually four years. Civil servants may be members of the *Landtage* except in North Rhine-Westphalia.

The executives of the Laender are cabinets headed by a minister-president. In Bremen and Hamburg the cabinet is called Senate and its chairman, the equivalent to the minister-president, is called Mayor (*Bürgermeister*) and Senate President in Bremen, but First Mayor (*Erster Bürgermeister*) in Hamburg.

Coalition governments are the rule in the Laender and have proven themselves quite stable although they have changed more often than the federal cabinet. In many Laender, between the Land government and the local authorities, there is an intermediate authority called Government District (*Regierungsbezirk*), headed by a Government President (*Regierungspräsident*) who is appointed by the Land government and subject to its direction. This institution has been criticized as unnecessary but it has prevailed. It is largely of Prussian origin though not confined only to the Laender carved out of the former Prussia.

On the whole the Laender of· the German Federal Republic

have more self-government than they had under the Weimar
Republic and of course under the Nazi regime. Although there
has been a certain trend towards greater centralization, they
have resisted it. For a while the trend was markedly political
because the Christian Democrats, although once the chief spokes-
men of federalism, wanted to dominate as many state governments as possible. This was especially true when the then Chancellor Konrad Adenauer desired a two-thirds majority in the
Bundesrat in order to effect certain constitutional changes. But
his move did not succeed and such attempts have become less
prominent, although national issues do tend to dominate Laender
elections more and more.

What protects the Laender from being submerged by the federal government is not so much their reserved powers under the
Constitution but rather the important position of the *Bundesrat*
and the vigilance of the Federal Constitutional Court in the
defense of "state's rights." Politically, the Laender governments
have developed a great deal of talent. This has been particularly
true of the Social Democrats who, long in opposition in the
national administration, found an outlet for their administrative
talents in the Laender governments. They also had an opportunity there to prove their worthiness to be called to power. But
among the Christian Democrats and the Free Democrats, Laender governments have been an outlet for many who were im-
patient with the many frustrations of national government,
especially when dominated by such imperious personalities as
Konrad Adenauer. Very often Laender governments have developed statesmen of the first magnitude. Particularly significant is
the present Federal Minister of Defense, Kai Uwe von Hassel,
who earned his chevrons as Prime Minister of Schleswig-Holl-
stein. Equally significant have been such men as Max Brauer
(now retired), and Wilhelm Kaisen, Mayors of Hamburg and
Bremen respectively; Georg August Zinn and the late Heinrich
Kopf, Prime Ministers of Hesse and Lower Saxony respectively;
and Heinrich Hellwege and Kurt Georg Kiesinger, Prime Ministers of Lower Saxony and Baden-Wuerttemberg. Nor would
this list be complete without a mention of Willy Brandt who
earned his national prominence as Lord Mayor of Berlin.

Although smaller parties, which have disappeared from the

Bundestag due to the operation of the 5 percent clause, have maintained themselves in several of the Laender, the increasing national trends in the elections foreshadow their doom on the Land and local level as well.

Local Government

As the federal government exercises regional functions through the Laender governments, so the latter exercise their local functions through local government. However, the local governments lack the protective device of anything equivalent to a *Bundesrat*.

Local government was relatively satisfactory at least before 1935. Although not entirely uniform, the prevailing system was that of an elected city council which elected a mayor, but the mayor had a very long term of office, certainly much longer than that of the council. Konrad Adenauer's mayoralty of Cologne from 1919 to 1933 is an example in point. In practice this meant that the mayor was a professional who had to blend with the directly elected councillors and did so generally with good results. The Nazis changed this in 1935 but the Allied Occupation Authorities did not immediately go back to the pre-Nazi system. Instead they attempted to introduce the systems to which they were accustomed at home. This was less true of the Americans than of the British and the French.

The British insisted on making both the mayor and the head of the counties (*Kreis*) the *Landrat,* that is, an elected political official, while vesting actual administrative control in a civil servant who in the municipalities became known as the city director (according to the size of the city, *Gemeindedirektor, Stadtdirektor,* or *Oberstadtdirektor*), For the *Kreis* the British created an elected *Landrat* and a professional *Kreis* director. The Germans did not like this system to which they were not accustomed and critics maintained that the separation between the political and administrative levels worked against the democratic development which was as yet untried.

In the French zone the French attempt to copy the *maire-adjoint* system in a foreign environment only raised incomprehension and led nowhere. The French system disappeared as soon as the French occupation ceased, but the British system has remained in the state of North Rhine-Westphalia.

The American zone went back to a modified version of the older, pre-Nazi, system.

Generally speaking, city government is regulated by Land law along fairly uniform lines. There are, however, considerable differences between the various Laender. Thus in Bavaria and Baden-Wuerttemberg we find what corresponds to a mayor-council type of government with the mayor in a strong position. He is elected directly by the people and in larger cities he is a full-time official with a six-year term. In Hesse the same system prevails on the whole but the law also permits a commission type of government and normally the *Bürgermeister* is elected by the council. In North Rhine-Westphalia, as already stated, the British system has remained.

A little more uniformity prevails on the district (*Kreis*) level. These districts are the main units of local government. In the case of more important towns, the town itself becomes a district, called urban district (*Stadtkreis*). It is in some ways comparable to the British county boroughs, and not subject to the jurisdiction of the district surrounding the city. The others are called rural districts (*Landkreis*). There are no uniform rules about when a city is to become a *Stadtkreis*.

Except for North Rhine-Westphalia, the most important official of the *Kreis* is the rural councillor (*Landrat*) whose position is combined with that of the mayor in the *Stadtkreise*. The *Landrat* used to be appointed but is now elected by the legislative council of the *Kreis*, the *Kreistag*. Only in the area of the former French zone is he still appointed, subject, however, to confirmation by the *Kreistag*. The *Landrat* is the chief executive of the *Kreis* and he appoints all officials. His salary is paid by the *Land* but the *Land* government has only limited control over him, as has been demonstrated by several unsuccessful attempts on the part of Land governments to get rid of *Landräte*.

Unlike the City Council, which meets frequently, the *Kreistag* meets only on occasion. In the interim a committee of the *Kreistag*, the *Kreisausschuss*, carries on much of its business and also serves the function of a commission in a commission type of municipal administration.

Because the municipalities are frequently small and their problems many, they find it useful to undertake certain joint or cooperative operations. Inasmuch as this coordination takes place within the confines of the *Landkreis*, it is regulated by law although additional intermunicipal agreements may be made on a voluntary basis. Such agreements may involve joint handling of certain problems, contracting, purchasing, etc. A more permanent joint authority between municipalities has been established in certain Laender under the name of administrative offices (*Ämter*). These *Ämter* are established for general governmental purposes, but there are also special intermunicipal authorities for specific purposes such as joint maintenance of utilities. These are called "common purposes associations" (*Zweckverbände*).

The functions which local government has to perform are very extensive, especially on the city level. Apart from the usual tasks of planning safety, health and welfare, German municipalities usually own and run their utilities and transportation systems and maintain cultural institutions.

The Government of West Berlin

It is customary that capital cities of countries are administered differently from other municipalities. This is true of Washington, London, Paris, and Vienna among others. This also occurred in Berlin when in 1912 the city was detached from the province of Brandenburg except for certain supervisory functions and achieved the status of a province in its own right. The city's charter of 1920 established the customary *Magistratsverfassung* which implies something between a mayor-council and a commission type of administration. Later on the position of the mayor was considerably strengthened. The city constitution also divided Berlin into 20 districts (*Bezirke*), each one with a charter similar to that of the city, and each with a district mayor and a district council.

The Russians who occupied the city first revived the pre-Nazi constitution but infiltrated the government heavily with Communists. When the four-power occupation was established, the United States occupied six districts, the British four, the French two, and the Russians eight. Although the city constitution nominally remained in force, considerable divergencies existed in the different sectors. This situation continued under the temporary charter of 1946.

The Russians walked out of the Allied Control Council on March 26, 1948, and on June 16, 1948, they left the four-power military government of Berlin known as the *Komandatura*. Shortly thereafter the famous Berlin blockade began and Communist pressure increased both inside and outside the city. On June 23, 1948, a Communist mob stormed the City Hall, which was located in the Russian sector; the City Council members from the Western sectors retreated to the West but the councillors of the Communist-controlled Socialist Unity Party (SED) refused to go along. Thus the split into two Berlins became an accomplished fact. In 1949 the three Western Allied powers enacted a "little occupation statute" which was the Berlin corollary to the occupation statute for the German Federal Republic, and on August 29, 1950, a permanent constitution for Berlin was adopted.

Berlin is now both a city and a Land, somewhat comparable to the status of Hamburg and Bremen. The Constitutional Court has clearly stated, "Berlin is a *Land* of the German Federal Republic." However, for reasons of international politics and in order not to give the Russians any pretext for interfering with Western right, the Allies suspended that part of the Constitution which would have fully incorporated Berlin into the German Federal Republic. Thus Berlin is a *Land* for internal purposes but it is not fully a Land of the German Federal Republic. Its status is kept deliberately vague by Germans and Allies alike. However, the German Federal Republic treats Berlin pretty much as if it were one of its Laender, and Berlin's hybrid status is underlined by the fact that it sends nonvoting members to both the *Bundestag* and the *Bundesrat*. Moreover, much of the city's income comes from federal government subsidies, and a number of federal authorities and courts are located in Berlin. Also, to underscore Berlin's unity with the Federal Republic, each session of the *Bundestag* has held at least one meeting in Berlin, and the Federal President is generally elected in Berlin.

The constitution of the city-state of Berlin parallels that of other Laender. There is a popularly elected House of Representatives *(Abgeordnetenhaus)*, composed of 200 members of whom only 127 are actually functioning because 73 seats are reserved for East Berlin as a gesture to demonstrate the unity of Berlin and the fact that the West Berlin city government considers itself a representative of the entire city. The House of Representatives is elected by proportional representation for four years. It in turn elects the chief executive who bears the title of Governing Mayor (*Regierender Bürgermeister*), and his deputy called *Bürgermeister*. It also elects a cabinet of 19 members called Senate. Mayor and cabinet must have the confidence of the House of Representatives and must resign if that confidence is withdrawn.

Each district elects a district government called *Bezirksamt* which is headed by a district mayor (*Bezirksbürgermeister*). These district mayors have established a council for mutual consultation and common action.

Although much of its prosperity is the result of subsidies from the Bonn government, West Berlin is a vibrant, exciting city, both economically and intellectually, especially in the arts. The prosperity and freedom of West Berlin stand in sharp contrast to the drabness and dictatorship of East Berlin. The erection of the wall between the two has brought regular transit to an end, but contacts remain and it is too easy to look from one sector into the other not to notice the enormous contrast. Although East Berlin has made slow progress and is treated as a showcase in East Germany, it remains living proof that the Communist regime works very badly indeed.

CHAPTER ELEVEN

A Concluding Look
at Germany

JUST TWENTY YEARS before this book was written, Germany lay in
an indescribable state of physical and moral ruin. Her cities were
devastated, her communications and supply system had completely collapsed, the flower of her manhood was in prison or
dead. Germany had ceased to exist as a country and was occupied by foreign soldiers whose governments had yet to decide
her ultimate fate. Those Germans who were asked what they
thought of their country's future were virtually unanimous in
their conviction that Germany was finished and would never
rise again.

Twenty years later, the German Federal Republic is not only
completely rebuilt, but the necessity to rebuild from total destruction has produced one of the most modern countries of
Europe. More than that, West Germany is an important and
respected member of the community of free nations. A great
deal of attention has been paid to this economic miracle which,
although a formidable achievement, is not unique. Belgium and
Holland, for instance, to mention only two, have made comparable recoveries without attracting the same attention. What
is perhaps even a greater miracle is the fact that the darkest
chapter in German history, the Nazi holocaust, although it came
to a fiery end such a relatively short time ago, nevertheless
seems both remote and unreal. And there are good indications
that the new democratic regime of the German Federal Republic,
in contrast to its Weimar predecessor, is firmly established. True,
history never sells insurance policies. There remains always the
possibility of a surprise. For example, who would have thought

a few years ago that the virtually "ungovernable" French would so willingly submit to the virtually unlimited rule of a single man, General de Gaulle, although the recent Presidential election of 1965 indicates that the French are having at least some second thoughts about his unlimited rule.

Yet in the German case there are quite a number of solid reasons for looking into the future with confidence. The very totality of the country's collapse in a way assured its future. The destruction, the occupation, left no doubt of the total military defeat of Germany. No "stab in the back" legend could grow on those ruins. Secondly, the end of World War II and the opening of the nuclear age also opened the age of the superpowers. The focus of world power status had moved away from Europe. A struggle for supremacy among the countries of that relatively small continent had now become devoid of all reason, and in the age of nuclear destruction no country whose territory was so small that it could be totally wiped out in a single attack could ever again aspire to world domination.

Thus, even while Germany's recent past lay heavily on her, Germany had in effect finished with her past, if for no other reason than that it failed to provide answers for the future. Certainly a good many old Nazis remained—how could it be otherwise? But even they failed to see how one could turn the clock back. To the world at large Naziism has remained an indescribable horror, a dark blemish on the entire human race and in particular on the German nation. But in Germany Naziism quickly became almost an absurdity, something which in retrospect made no sense. Perhaps no greater proof of this extraordinary development can be found than the continued inability of the older generation to explain the past in terms meaningful to their children.

As a result, the new democratic order was established without resistance—not because all Germans had suddenly become enthusiastic democrats overnight, but rather because there was a vacuum in which almost anything that worked could be established. Fortunately for the world and for Germany, German democracy did work, thanks to the prudence and moderation of her leaders and to the wisdom of the Western powers which in various ways furthered this development. If the United States is primarily responsible for this assistance during the earlier period of the fledgling Federal Republic, Franco-German reconciliation which brought Germany back into "Europe" deserves similar credit at a later stage, though well before General de Gaulle came to power in Paris.

Today Germany is a profoundly different nation from what she was a quarter or a half century ago. The bitter cleavages and hatreds on which extremist movements feed are absent from the German scene. Although there are great differences in wealth, there is no real poverty. There are no real fundamentally opposed social forces, and the political parties have drawn the proper conclusions from the situation by endeavoring to represent a cross section of the population rather than specific classes, groups, or regions.

However, there is one cleavage among the people which, as a shrewd observer, Peter D. G. Brown, has remarked, works in favor of Germany's democratic future: it is the split between the younger and the older generations. In this there lies much hope and some uncertainty.

In contrast to their fathers and forefathers, Germany's young people cannot easily be distinguished from the youth of other parts of free Europe. The enormous mobility of our age has, as Robert Schuman so wisely foresaw, "devaluated" national frontiers. If Henry Ford brought about a revolution in America, so the Volkswagen and even smaller types of transportation including the motor scooters have brought similar revolutions to Europe. Today's younger German generation roves all over the continent, it recognizes little specific differences in styles of architecture or of living, and its literature is now wholly international. Like most of the youth of Europe it is an intensely practical, basically unideological youth. The care with which the older generations once established national distinctions and separations makes little sense to these young people. This is why even the most honest attempts by their elders to explain their history and their guilt meets with massive incomprehension. They have "to a large degree condemned and rejected the values which their parents and grandparents had so highly prized." (Brown)

This is all to the good, but there are some uncertainties. Political life in Germany is still dominated by the older generation.

The German *Bundestag* is the "oldest" in Europe. The average age of members of the Fourth *Bundestag* (1961–1965) was slightly above 52 years. Its two youngest members were born in the year Hitler came to power, in 1933. The 1965 elections improved the situation somewhat; the average age descended—to 50.

It is not that the political parties reject the participation of youth; quite the contrary. Rather is it the youth which has not taken to political life. Politics still does not have a respectable sound in Germany, and the young generation views it with a suspicion which, while perhaps not entirely unhealthy, is not a constructive attitude for the future. Perhaps one reason for this attitude is the fact that Germany's democracy was not a German achievement or an achievement by Germans, but rather the result of external circumstances to which, to be sure, many distinguished Germans contributed greatly. But there is no German folklore surrounding the birth of the Federal Republic.

If there is one ideal which has received broad acceptance among Germany's youth it is the idea of a united Europe. But in a way this ideal was too vague and many were too optimistic in their belief in an early realization for disappointment not to have set in. That disappointment is a fact. A united Europe is clearly not just around the corner. Yet a separate German identity is made difficult by the previously discussed impact of Germany's division. Hence a good part of Germany's youth finds itself in a kind of vacuum over which it reflects and sometimes agonizes.

Germany's democratic institutions are not affected by this agony because the issues at hand do not put them in question. But neither are they capable of producing an answer because Germany's future course is largely determined by factors which lie outside the German Federal Republic.

Thus Germany's future is inextricably intertwined with the future of free Europe and of the Atlantic family of free nations. If Germany is accorded a place of equality and full partnership in both the European and the Atlantic spheres, her youth can find a full range of opportunity for the expression of her aspirations and of her identity even if the day of German reunification remains in the distant future. If Germany, however, is cast adrift, isolated in some sort of ill-conceived "neutralization," if she becomes a country of lesser rights, then it is predictable that a generation which was born after Hitler's death and which therefore cannot retain a sentiment of responsibility for his misdeeds, will once again question the very foundation on which the Republic has been established. In that case, while a return to Naziism would seem unlikely and incongruous even under those circumstances, nobody could tell where Germany might go.

Happily, there is every reason to believe that the lessons of the past have been learned sufficiently both in Germany and in the West to exclude such a catastrophe. Thus there is good cause for hope that Germany, in both her foreign and her domestic affairs, will remain a member of the West European and Atlantic family in the clear recognition that that family and Germany need one another.

A SELECTED BIBLIOGRAPHY

GERMANY has been a "problem area" for some time, and hence a large literature on it exists. In the list which follows below, the author has concentrated on the standard works in general, and on more recent works in particular, especially when dealing with contemporary problems. Preference, where possible, has been given to works in the English language, but the German language literature is now so extensive and significant that a number of important works and articles have been included in the hope that at least some of the readers will find them useful. For those who wish to study German government and politics more thoroughly, it goes without saying that a good knowledge of the German language is indispensable. The somewhat less voluminous but significant literature on Germany in the French language has been omitted except for the important works by Alfred Grosser which have been translated either into English or German. At any rate, this selected bibliography is presented as an initial guide, not as a substitute for serious bibliographical work by persons wishing to undertake penetrating studies.

The leading German newspapers are *Frankfurter Allgemeine Zeitung* of Frankfurt, *Süddeutsche Zeitung* of Munich, and *Die Welt* of Hamburg and Berlin, but in the opinion of this author the German language paper with the most penetrating (though somewhat conservative) commentary on Germany is the *Neue Zürcher Zeitung* of Zurich, Switzerland. There are numerous excellent periodicals such as *Europa-Archiv, Aussenpolitik, Die politische Meinung, Politische Vierteljahrschrift, Politische Studien, Der Monat, Frankfurter Hefte,* and many more. A useful collection of assorted data may be found in *Facts About Germany,* 4th ed., Wiesbaden, 1962, commissioned by the Federal Government. More extensive data are found in the official *Statistisches Jahrbuch,* an annual publication, and a brief version in English, *Handbook of Statistics.*

GENERAL HISTORY

Baraclough, G., *The Origins of Modern Germany,* 2nd ed., Oxford, 1949.

Conze, Werner, *Die Deutsche Nation; Ergebnis der Geschichte,* Goettingen, 1963.

Craig, Gordon, *From Bismarck to Adenauer,* Baltimore, 1958.

Dill, Marshall, Jr., *Germany: A Modern History,* Ann Arbor, 1961.

Hawgood, John A., *The Evolution of Germany*, London, 1955.

Holborn, Hajo, *A History of Modern Germany*, New York, 1959.

Pollack, James K., and M. Thomas, et al., *Germany in Power and Eclipse*, New York, 1952.

Taylor, A. J. P., *The Course of German History*, New York, 1946.

Valentin, Veit, *The German People*, New York, 1946.

THE WEIMAR REPUBLIC

Blachly, F. F., and M. E. Oatman, *The Government and Administration of Germany*, Baltimore, 1928.

Bracher, Karl Dietrich, *Die Auflösung der Weimarer Republik*, 2nd ed., Stuttgart-Düsseldorf, 1957.

Brecht, Arnold, *Federalism and Regionalism in Germany*, New York, 1945.

Brunet, René, *The New German Constitution* (trans. by J. Gollomb), New York, 1922.

Eyck, Erich, *A History of the Weimar Republic* (trans. by H. P. Hanson and R. G. L. Waite), Cambridge, Mass., 1963.

Halperin, William S., *Germany Tried Democracy*, New York, 1946.

Hermens, F. A., *Democracy or Anarchy*, Notre Dame, Ind., 1941.

Hertzmann, Lewis, *Rightwing Opposition in the Weimar Republic, 1918–1924*, Nebraska University, 1964.

Rosenberg, Arthur, *A History of the German Republic*, London, 1936.

Scheele, Godfrey, *The Weimar Republic: Overture to the Third Reich*, London, 1946.

Sturmthal, A. F., *The Tragedy of European Labor 1918–1939*, New York, 1943.

THE NAZI PERIOD

Bracher, K. D., W. Sauer, and Gerhard Schulz, "Die nationalsozialistische Machtergreifung," *Schriften des. Institut für Politische Wissenschaft*, vol. 14, 1960.

Bullock, Alan L. C., *Hitler, a Study in Tyranny*, rev. ed., New York, 1958.

Butler, R. D., *The Roots of National Socialism*, New York, 1942.

Dulles, Allen W., *Germany's Underground*, New York, 1947.

Epstein, Klaus, *The German Opposition to Hitler*, Chicago, 1962.

Fraenkel, Ernst, *The Dual State: A Contribution to the Theory of Dictatorship*, New York, 1941.

Frank, Anne, *The Diary of a Young Girl* (trans. by M. Mooyaat), New York, 1952.

Gallin, Mary Alice, *German Resistance to Hitler; Ethical and Religious Factors*, Washington, D.C., 1962.

Gisevius, E. B., *To the Bitter End*, Boston, 1947.

Heiden, Konrad, *Der Fuehrer*, London, 1944.

Heiden, Konrad, *A History of National Socialism*, New York, 1935.

Kogon, Eugen, *Der SS Staat: Das System der deutschen Konzentrationslager*, Munich, 1946; *The Theory and Practice of Hell: The German Concentration Camps and the System Behind Them* (trans. by H. Norden), New York, 1950.

Leber, Annedore, and Freya Gräfin von Moltke, *Für und wider; Entscheidungen in Deutschland 1918–1945*, Berlin, 1961.

Neumann, Franz, *Behemoth: The Structure and Practice of National Socialism*, New York, 1942.

Pollock, James K., *The Government of Greater Germany*, New York, 1938.

Rauschnigg, Hermann, *The Voice of Destruction*, New York, 1940.

Roberts, Stephen H., *The House That Hitler Built*, New York, 1938.

Rothfels, Hans, *The German Opposition to Hitler*, Hinsdale, Ill., 1948.

Royce, Hans, compiler, supplemented by Erich Zimmermann and Hans-Adolf Jacobsen, *Germans against Hitler, July 20, 1944*, Bonn, 1960.

Shirer, William L., *The Rise and Fall of the Third Reich; A History of Nazi Germany*, New York, 1960.

Szaz, Z. M., "The ideological precursor of National Socialism," *Western Political Quarterly*, vol. 16, no. 4 (Dec. 1963), pp. 924–945.

THE RECONSTRUCTION OF GERMANY

Almond, Gabriel A., *The Struggle for Democracy in Germany*, Chapel Hill, N.C., 1949.

Balfour, Michael, and John Mair, *Four Power Control in Germany and Austria, 1945–1946*, Oxford, 1956.

Clay, Lucius D., *Decision in Germany*, New York, 1950.

Ebsworth, Raymond, *Restoring Democracy in Germany: The British Contribution*, New York, 1962.

Friedman, W., *The Allied Military Government of Germany*, London, 1947.

Friedrich, C. J. and Associates, *American Experiences in Military Government in World War II*, New York, 1948.

Golay, John F., *The Founding of the Federal Republic of Germany*, Chicago, 1958.

Grosser, Alfred, *The Federal Republic of Germany, A Concise History* (trans. by N. Aldrich), New York, 1964.

Grosser, Alfred, *La République de Bonn*, Paris, 1958.

Grosser, Alfred, *Colossus Again: Western Germany from Defeat to Rearmament*, New York, 1955.

Herz, John H., "The Fiasco of De-Nazification in Germany," *Political Science Quarterly*, vol. 63 (1948), pp. 569–594.

Hiscocks, Richard, *Democracy in Western Germany*, London, 1957.

Holborn, Hajo, *Military Government Organization and Politics*, New York, 1947.

Kohn, H., "Out of Catastrophe: Germany 1945–1960," *Review of Politics* (Apr. 1960), pp. 163–174.

Litchfield, E., and Associates, *Governing Postwar Germany*, Ithaca, N.Y., 1953.

Merkl, Peter H., *The Origin of the West German Republic*, New York, 1963.

Nettl, J. P., "A Decade of Post-War Germany," *Political Quarterly*, vol. 27 (1956), pp. 162–175.

"Postwar Reconstruction in Western Germany," *Annals of the American Academy of Political and Social Science*, November, 1948 (entire issue).

Wallich, H. C., *Mainsprings of the German Revival*, New Haven, 1955.

Zink, Harold, *The United States in Germany, 1944–1955*, New York, 1957.

Zink, Harold, *American Military Government in Germany*, New York, 1947.

POLITICAL PARTIES AND POLITICS

Baerwald, F., "Die Verbände in der Demokratie der Gegenwart," *Zeitschrift für Politik*, vol. 10, no. 1 (1963), pp. 54–62.

Barnes, S. H., F. Grace, J. K. Pollock, and P. W. Sperlich, "The German party system and the 1961 federal election," *American Political Science Review*, vol. 56, no. 4 (1962), pp. 899–914.

Bergsträsser, Ludwig, *Geschichte der politischen Parteien in Deutschland*, 10th ed. Munich, 1960.

Besson, W., "Regierung und Opposition in der Deutschen Politik," *Politische Vierteljahresschrift*, vol. 3, no. 3 (1962), pp. 225–241.

Bölling, Klaus, *Republic in Suspense*, New York, 1964.

Bonn, Dr. Ulrich, *Parteifinanzierung in Deutschland*, Cologne, 1962.

Brandt, Willy (as told to L. Lania), *My Road to Berlin*, New York, 1960.

Braunthal, Gerard, "The Free Democratic Party in West Germany," *Western Political Quarterly*, vol. 13 (1960), pp. 332–348.

Breitling, R., "Das Geld in der deutschen Parteipolitik," *Politische Vierteljahresschrift*, vol. 2, no. 4 (1962), pp. 348–363.

Chalmers, Douglas A., *The Social Democratic Party of Germany: From Working Class Movement to Modern Political Party*, New Haven, 1964.

Domes, Jurgen, *Mehrheitsfraktion und Bundesregierung*, Cologne, 1963.

Eberlein, K. D., "Die Wahlentscheidung vom 17. Sept. 1962, ihre Ursachen und Wirkung," *Zeitschrift für Politik*, vol. 9, no. 3 (1962), pp. 237–257.

Edinger, Lewis J., "Post Totalitarian Leadership: elites in the

German Federal Republic," *American Political Science Review*, vol. 54, no. 1 (1960), pp. 58–82.

Epstein, K., "Three American Studies of German Socialism," *World Politics*, vol. 11, no. 4 (1959), pp. 629–651.

Eschenburg, Theodor, *Herrschaft der Verbände?* Stuttgart, 1963.

Flechtheim, Ossip K., *Dokumente zur parteipolitischen Entwicklung in Deutschland seit 1945*, 3 vols., Berlin, 1962–63.

Freund, L., "The De-Marxification of the Social Democratic Party of Germany," *Modern Age*, vol. 5, no. 3 (1961), pp. 290–298.

Grebing, H., "Hundert Jahre S. P. D.: zwischen Tradition und Fortschritt," *Politische Studien*, vol. 14, no. 151 (1963), pp. 529–542.

Grundmann, W., "Die Finanzierung der politische Parteien," *Zeitschrift der gesammten Staatswissenschaften*, vol. 115, no. 1 (1959), pp. 113–130.

Hamann, A., "Das Recht auf Opposition und seine Geltung im Ausserparlementarischen Bereich," *Politische Vierteljahresschrift*, vol. 3, no. 3 (1962), pp. 242–255.

Hartenstein, W., and K. Liepelt, "Party members and party voters in Western Germany," *Acta sociologica*, vol. 6, nos. 1–2 (1962), pp. 43–52.

Heberle, R., "Parliamentary Government and Political Parties in West Germany," *Canadian Journal of Economic and Political Science*, vol. 28, no. 3 (1962), pp. 417–423.

Heidenheimer, Arnold J., "Der starke Regierungschef und das Parteien-System: der Kanzler-Effekt in der Bundesrepublik," *Politische Vierteljahresschrift*, vol. 2, no. 3 (1961), pp. 241–262.

Heidenheimer, Arnold J., *Adenauer and the CDU. The Rise of the Leader and the Integration of the Party*, The Hague, 1960.

Heidenheimer, Arnold J., "Foreign Policy and Party Discipline in the C.D.U.," *Parliamentary Affairs*, vol. 13, no. 1 (1959–1960) pp. 70–87.

Heidenheimer, Arnold J., "Federalism and the Party System, the Case of West Germany," *American Political Science Review*, vol. 52 (1958), pp. 809–828.

Heidenheimer, Arnold J., "German Party Finance. The C.D.U.,"

American Political Science Review, vol. 51 (1957), pp. 369–385.

Heimar, B., "Inner Struggle in the German Social Democracy," *International Politics*, vol. 4 (1959), pp. 82–87.

von der Heydte, F. H. and K. Sacherl, *Soziologie der deutschen Parteien*, Munich, 1955.

Hirsch-Weber, Wolfgang, *Gewerkschaften in der Politik, von der Massenstreikdebatte bis zum Kampf um das Mitbestimmungsrecht*, Cologne, 1959.

Johnson, N., "The era of Adenauer and after," *Parliamentary Affairs*, vol. 17, no. 1 (1963–1964), pp. 31–49.

Kerr, Clark, "The Trade Union Movement and the Redistribution of Power in Post-War Germany," *Quarterly Journal of Economics*, vol. 68 (1954), pp. 535–564.

Kitzinger, U. W., *German Electoral Politics, A Study of the 1957 Campaign*, Oxford, 1960.

Kitzinger, U. W., "The West German Electoral Law," *Parliamentary Affairs*, vol. 11 (1958), pp. 220–237.

Knütter, Hans-Helmuth, *Ideologien des Rechtsradikalismus im Nachkriegsdeutschland* (Bonner Historische Forschungen, vol. 19), Bonn, 1961.

Kohn, Hans, *Nationalism, its Meaning and History*, Princeton, 1955.

Landauer, Carl, *European Socialism, A History of Ideas and Movements from the Industrial Revolution to Hitler's Seizure of Power*, 2 vols., Berkeley, 1959.

Merkl, Peter H., *Germany: Yesterday and Tomorrow*, New York, 1965.

Molt, P., "Wertvorstellungen in Politik: Zur Frage der Entideologierung der deutschen Parteien," *Politische Vierteljahresschrift*, vol. 4, no. 4 (1963), pp. 350–368.

Mommsen, Wilhelm, *Deutsche Parteiprogramme*, Munich, 1960.

Neumann, Sigmund, "Germany, Changing Patterns and Lasting Problems," in S. Neumann, ed., *Modern Political Parties*, Chicago, 1956, pp. 354–392.

Oppen, B. R. von, "The end of the Adenauer era," *World Today*, vol. 19, no. 8 (1963), pp. 343–352.

Osterrath, F. and D. Schuster, *Chronik der deutschen Sozialdemokratie*, Hanover, 1963.

Pikart, E., "Probleme der Deutschen Parlamentspraxis," *Zeitschrift für Politik,* vol. 9, no. 3 (1962), pp. 201–211.

Pinney, Edward, *Federalism, Bureaucracy, and Party Politics in West Germany,* Chapel Hill, N.C., 1963.

Pulzer, P. G. J., "Western Germany and the three-party system," *Political Quarterly,* vol. 33, no. 4 (1962), pp. 414–426.

Rueckert, G. L. and W. Crane, "C.D.U. deviancy in the German Bundestag," *Journal of Politics,* vol. 24, no. 3 (1962), pp. 477–488.

Sauer, W., "Das Problem der deutschen Nationalstaaten," *Politische Vierteljahresschrift,* vol. 3, no. 2 (1962), pp. 159–186.

Schwarz-Liebermann von Wahlendorf, Hans Albrecht, *Struktur und Funktion der sogenannten Zweiten Kammer; eine Studie zum Problem der Gewaltenteilung,* Tübingen, 1958.

Speier, Hans, and W. P. Davison, *West German Leadership and Foreign Policy,* New York, 1957.

Stahl, Walter, ed., *The Politics of Postwar Germany,* New York, 1963.

Treue, Wolfgang, *Die Deutschen Parteien,* Wiesbaden, 1961.

Wildenmann, Rudolf, *Partei und Fraktion,* Meisenheim, 1955.

Williams, J. E., "Federal Elections in West Germany," *World Today,* vol. 17, no. 12 (1961), pp. 512–518.

Wössner, J., "Parlamentarische Mehrheit und politische Autorität," *Politische Studien,* vol. 14, no. 150 (1963), pp. 418–427.

THE INSTITUTIONS OF GOVERNMENT

Adenauer, Konrad, "The Development of Parliamentary Institutions in Germany since 1945," *Parliamentary Affairs,* vol. 9 (1947), pp. 1–8.

Alleman, F. R., *Bonn ist nicht Weimar,* Cologne, 1956.

Bode, Ingeborg, *Ursprung und Begriff der parlamentarischen Opposition* (Sozialwissenschaftliche Studien, Heft 3), Stuttgart, 1962.

Braunthal, G., "Federalism in Germany: the broadcasting controversy," *Journal of Politics,* vol. 24, no. 3 (1962), pp. 545–561.

Dietze, G., "The Federal Republic of Germany: an Evaluation After Ten Years," *Journal of Politics,* vol. 22, no. 1 (1960), pp. 112–147.

Ellwein, Thomas, *Das Regierungssystem der Bundesrepublik Deutschland*, Cologne, 1963.

Eschenburg, Theodor, *Herrschaft der Verbände?*, Stuttgart, 1963.

Eschenburg, Theodor, *Staat und Gesellschaft in Deutschland*, 3rd ed., Munich, 1963.

Eschenburg, Theodor, *Institutionelle Sorgen in der Bundesrepublik; Politische Aufsätze 1957–1961*, Stuttgart, 1961.

Freund, G., *Germany Between Two Worlds*, New York, 1961.

Frowein, Jochen, *Die selbständige Bundesaufsicht nach dem Grundgesetz* (Bonner Rechtswissenschaftliche Abhandlingen, Band 50), Bonn, 1961.

Füsslein, R. W., "Die Stabilität des Regierungssystems under der Geltung des Grundgesetzes," *Zeitschrift der Politik*, vol. 6, no. 4 (1959), pp. 310–317.

Grosser, Alfred, *Die Bonner Demokratie*, Düsseldorf, 1960 (trans. by Dr. Marlin Steinert, La démocratie de Bonn).

Heidenheimer, Arnold J., *The Governments of Germany*, New York, 1961.

Hirsch-Weber, Wolfgang, *The Shaping of Post-war Germany*, Cologne, 1959.

Horne, Alistair, *Return to Power*, New York, 1956.

Johnson, N. "Questions in the Bundestag," *Parliamentary Affairs*, vol. 16, no. 1 (1962), pp. 22–34.

Kirchheimer, O., "German Democracy in the 1950's," *World Politics*, vol. 13 (1961) pp. 254–266.

Kürschners Volkshandbuch; Deutscher Bundestag, 4. Wahlperiode 1961, Darmstadt, 1962.

Lechner, Hans, and Klaus Hülshoff, *Parlament und Regierung*, 2nd ed., Munich, 1958.

Loewenberg, G., "Parlamentarism in West Germany: the functioning of the Bundestag," *American Political Science Review*, vol. 55 (1961), pp. 87–102.

Maunz, Theodor, and Günter Durig, *Grundgesetz*, Munich, 1963 & 1964.

Maunz, Theodor, *Deutsches Staatsrecht*, 9th ed., Munich, 1959.

Merkl, Peter M., "Executive-Legislative Federalism in West Germany," *American Political Science Review*, vol. 53 (1959), pp. 732–741.

Model, Otto, *Staatsbürger Taschenbuch*, Munich, 1963.

Munch, F., *Die Bundesregierung*, Frankfurt, 1954.

Neumann, Robert G., *European and Comparative Government*, 3rd ed., New York, 1960.

Neunreither, K., "Federalism and West German Bureaucracy," *Political Studies*, vol. 7, no. 3 (1959), pp. 233–245.

Neunreither, K., "Politics and Bureaucracy in the West German Bundesrat," *American Political Science Review*, vol. 53, no. 3 (1959), pp. 713–731.

Olzog, G., "Von der Zukunft der Vergangenheit: 10 Jahre Bonner Grundgesetz," *Politische Studien*, vol. 10, no. 109 (1959), pp. 285–296.

Pinney, E. L., "Latent and Manifest Bureaucracy in the West German Parliament: the case of the Bundesrat," *Midwest Journal of Political Science*, vol. 6, no. 2 (1962), pp. 149–164.

Poittie, T., "The Federal German Parliament," *Parliamentary Affairs*, vol. 10 (1956–1957), pp. 57–62.

Schmidt, W., "Das Verhältnis von Bund und Ländern im demokratischen Bundesstaat des Grundgesetzes," *Archiv für öffentliches Recht*, vol. 87, no. 3 (1962), pp. 253–296.

Schuster, Rudolf, *Deutschlands staatliche Existenz im Widerstreit politischer und rechtlicher Gesichtspunkte 1945–1963*, Munich, 1963.

Simons, Hans, "The Bonn Constitution and its Government" in H. Morgenthau (ed.), *Germany and the Future of Europe*, Chicago, 1951.

Speier, Hans, and W. P. Davison, etc., *West German Leadership and Foreign Policy*, New York, 1957.

Thieme, Werner, *Der öffentliche Dienst in der Verfassungsordnung des Grundgesetzes*, Göttingen, 1961.

Ullman, R. K. and S. King-Hall, *German Parliaments: A Study of the Development of Representative Institutions in Germany*, New York, 1955.

Zöller, Josef Othmar, *Rückblick auf die Gegenwart: Die Entstehung der Kanzlerdemokratie*, Stuttgart, 1964.

LAW AND JUSTICE

Baade, Hans W., "Social Science Evidence and the Federal Constitutional Court of West Germany," *Journal of Politics*, vol. 23, no. 3 (1961), pp. 421–461.

Das Bundesverfassungsgericht, Karlsruhe, 1963 (by the Court).

Cole, T., "The Role of Labor Courts in Western Germany," *Journal of Politics*, vol. 18 (1956), pp. 479–498.

Cole, T., "The West German Federal Constitutional Court: An Evaluation After Six Years," *Journal of Politics*, vol. 20 (1958), pp. 278–307.

Cole, T., "Three Constitutional Courts: A Comparison," *American Political Science Review*, vol. 53, no. 4 (1959), pp. 963–984.

Friesenhahn, Ernst, *Die Verfassungsgerichtsbarkeit in der Bundesrepublik Deutschland*, Cologne, 1963.

Leibholz, Gerhard, "Die Stellung des Bundesverfassungsgerichts im Rahmen des Bonner Grundgesetzes," *Politische Vierteljahresschrift*, vol. 3, no. 1 (1962), pp. 113–125.

Leibholz, Gerhard, "The Federal Constitutional Court in Germany and the 'Southwest' Case," *American Political Science Review*, vol. 46, (1955), pp. 805–839.

Loewenstein, Karl, "Justice," in Litchfield and Associates, *Governing Postwar Germany*, Ithaca, N.Y., 1953, pp. 236–262.

Loewenstein, Karl, "Reconstruction of the Administration of Justice in American-Occupied Germany," *Harvard Law Review*, vol. 60 (1948), pp. 419–467.

McWhinney, Edward, "The German Federal Constitutional Court and the Communist Party Decision," *Indiana Law Journal*, vol. 36 (1959), pp. 546 ff.

Nagel, H., "Judicial Review in Germany," *American Journal of Comparative Law*, vol. 3 (1954), pp. 233–241.

Rheinstein, Max, "Approach to German Law," *Indiana Law Journal*, vol. 34 (1959), pp. 546–558.

Rupp, Hans G., "Judicial Review in the Federal Republic of Germany," *American Journal of Comparative Law*, vol. 9 (1960), pp. 29–47.

Schmertzing, Wolfgang P. von, *Outlawing the Communist Party, A Case History*, London, 1957.

Wunderlich, Frieda, *German Labor Courts*, Chapel Hill, N.C., 1946.

GERMANY AND THE WORLD

Brentano, Heinrich von, *Germany and Europe*, trans. by E. Fitzgerald, New York, 1964.

Brentano, Heinrich von, *Deutschland, Europa und die Welt, Reden zur Deutschen Aussenpolitik*, Bonn, 1962.

Butz, Otto, *Germany: Dilemma for American Foreign Policy*, New York, 1962.

Deutsch, Karl, and Lewis Edinger, *Germany Rejoins the Powers: Mass Opinion, Interest Groups and Elites in Contemporary German Foreign Policy*, Stanford, 1959.

Deutsche Politik 1961, Tätigkeitsbericht der Bundesregierung, Presse und Informationsamt der Bundesregierung (no date).

Erhard, Ludwig, *Deutsche Wirtschafts-politik*, Düsseldorf, Vienna, 1962. English translation by J. A. Arengo-Jones and D. J. S. Thomson, *The Economics of Success*, London, 1963.

Erler, Fritz, *Ein Volk sucht seine Sicherheit*, Frankfurt-on-Main, 1961.

Grewe, Wilhelm G., *Deutsche Aussenpolitik der Nachkriegszeit*, Stuttgart, 1960.

Hubatsch, Walther, Johanna Schomerus, and Werner John, *Die Deutsche Frage*, Würzburg, 1961.

Jasper, Karl, *Freiheit und Wiedervereinigung: Über Aufgaben deutscher Politik*, Munich, 1960.

Robson, Charles B., ed., *Berlin: Pivot of German Destiny*, Chapel Hill, N.C., 1960.

Schroeder, Gerhard, *Wir brauchen eine heile Welt: Politik in und für Deutschland*, Düsseldorf-Vienna, 1963. English translation by D. J. S. Thompson, *Decision for Europe*, London, 1964.

Speier, Hans, *Divided Berlin: The Anatomy of Soviet Political Blackmail*, New York, 1961.

Stolper, Wolfgang F., *Germany Between East and West*, Washington, 1960.

INDEX

Abs, H. J., 79
Absolutism, 5
Adams, Sherman, 111
Act, 78; legislative, executive, 78
Adenauer, Konrad, 16, 45–54, 56, 62, 65–66, 69, 71, 73, 76–77, 81, 84, 89, 104–111, 140, 141, 151, 157–158
Adenauer cabinet, 55, 57, 67; policy, 61
Administration, American, 33; British, 33; French 33; Truman-Acheson, 54; municipal, 92
Ahlen program, 45
Allied authorities, 24
Allied Control Council, 161
Allied High Commission, 34; military command, 24
Allies, 9, 20–21, 34, 60, 161; Western, 41, 54
Alsace-Lorraine, 82
Alsatians, 38
Amnesty, 26
Anglo-Saxons, 2
Anti-Semitism, 12
Arbitrariness, 6
Archbishop, 3
Armistice, 23–24
Army discipline, 132; German, 57, 121; Napoleonic, 6; professional, 5; Soviet, 21
Arnold Karl, 46, 66
Arrest, 96, 132
Assembly, Federal, 104; French, 104; protection of rights of, 96
Association, business, 81; General German Workers, 38; professional, 81
Asylum, 99
Atlantic Alliance, 57, 64, 67, 75
Auschwitz (Oświęcim), 15
Austria, 4
Authoritarianism, 6–7

Authorities, Allied Occupation, 158; intermunicipal, 160; International of the Ruhr, 33

Backbencher, 130
Bad Godesberg, 62
Baden, 65
Baden, Prince Max of, 9, 40
Baden-Wuerttemberg, 70, 77, 90, 118, 155–156, 159
Bail, 96
Ballot, 104, 106, 123, 127
Bar, 144
Barzel, Rainer, 58, 73–74, 140
Basic Law (Grundgesetz), 35, 88, 90–91, 99, 105, 119, 129
Bavaria, 32, 47, 58, 70, 72, 88, 90, 97, 118, 159; Constitution, 155–156
Bebel, August, 38
Beerhall Putsch, 12
Belgium, 33
Berg, Fritz, 79
Bergen-Belsen, 15, 25
Berlin, 22, 44, 59, 64, 89; blockade of, 161; charter of, 160–161; constitution, 161; Council, 161; councillors, 161; district (Bezirke), 160; district council, 160; district mayor, 160; income, 161; Land, 161; legal position, 125; legislature, 125; mayor, 62, 160; military government (Kommandatura), 161
Bill, 137; first, second, and third readings, 134; fourth reading, 135
Bismarck, Prince Otto von, 7–8, 37–39, 87, 119
"Black Reichswehr," 10
Blank, Theodor, 57, 133
"Blood and iron" image, 8
Bluecher, Franz, 66
Boeckler, Hans, 80
Bonn, 79, 89, 126–127, 141, 155

For the convenience of the reader, political parties have been grouped together under the heading, "Political parties."

181

Border control, 90
Brandenburg, 160; Margrave of, 3
Brandt, Willy, 62–64, 157
Brauer, Max, 157
Bremen, 62, 70, 88, 90, 97, 118, 156
Brentano, Heinrich von, 51, 55–56, 140
British, 158, 160; Isles, 2
Brown, P. D. G., 165
Bruening, Heinrich, 13–14, 40
Buchenwald, 15, 25
Bucher, Ewald, 145
Bulgaria, 21
Bundesrat (Federal Council), 91, 131, 134–138, 149, 157–158, 161; appointment, 118; chairmanship, 119; composition, 118; consent, 119; influence, 119, 121; majority, 120; power, 119; rulings, 122; veto, 119–121
Bundestag (Federal Diet), 42, 44, 55–56, 63–64, 68–69, 73, 77–78, 93, 102, 105, 107, 111, 122, 123, 127, 130–138, 145, 147, 149–151, 158, 161; age of members, 166; committees, 120; deputies, 80, 128, 129; Fraktion (parliamentary group), 129; majority, 103, 106, 120; member, 106; president, 46
Bureau of the Budget, 113
Bureaucracy, 7, 60, 154; federal, 91; Land, 91

Cabinet, 56, 73, 102, 107, 110, 134; appointment, 106; candidate, 130; crisis, 105; decision, 112; deliberation, 112; meeting, 111; member, 106, 140; minister, 74
Campaign, 70, 81
CARE, 32
Carstens, Karl, 131
Categorical imperative, 95
Capital, 89
Case, civil, 146; criminal, 146
Catholic, 4, 47, 149; Church, 38
Catholics, 38, 44, 116
Caucus decisions (Franktionszwang), 129
Cement, 49
Centralization, 138, 157

(Continued)
Century, 2
Chancellor, 7, 11, 47–48, 53, 57, 72, 74, 102, 105–106, 109, 136, 137, 141; death of, 103; democracy, 108; resignation, 103, 111; responsibility, 11, 112
Chancellorship, 51–53, 56, 62, 77, 110
Charlemagne, 2
Christianization, 4
Churchill, Winston, 19, 23, 50
Cities, Hanseatic, 90
Citizen soldier, 132
Citizenship loss, 97
City Council, 158–159; director, 158; government, 159
Civil defense, 90
Civil liberties, 95, 100
Civil rights, 98–99, 150
Civil Service, 5, 117, 120, 154; Act (1953), 114; commission, 115; educational prerequisites, 115; efficiency, 114; elevated, 115; examinations, 115; figures (1963), 115; higher, 115; middle, 115; professional (Berufsbeamtentum), 114; reform, 115; retirement, 116; simple, 115
Civil war, European, 84
Coal, 49
Coalition, 45–46, 72, 106, 137; agreement, 55; government, 66–67, 76, 156; party, 68; post-election (1965), 77
Collaboration, 65
College, American, 115
Cologne, 44, 48, 158; Principles of, 45
Commission, federal personnel, 115
Commissioner, supervisory, 91
Committee, 128, 133–134, 138–139; chairmanship, 131; composition, 131; defense, 132–133; meeting, 130; permanent, 132
Common Market, 56, 84
Commonwealth, 2
Communism, 54, 60
Communist regime, 162
Communists, 6, 13–14, 16, 27–30, 41, 59, 63, 83, 160–162

Community, 98; European Atomic Energy (EURATOM), 84; European Coal and Steel (ECSC), 56, 62, 84; European Economic (Common Market), 51, 56, 84; European Defense (EDC), 103–104

Compensation (Aufwandsentschädigung), 128

Compromise, 74; legal, 143

Concentration camps, 15, 25, 60, 99

Confederation, 87

Conference committee, 120, 121, 135

Conference, Permanent, of the Ministers of Education, 122

Conscription, military, 90

Conspirators, 16–17

Constance, University of, 94

Constitution, 33, 35, 48, 52, 89, 91–92, 99, 105, 108–109, 127, 132, 136–137, 144, 151–152, 157; amendment, 96, 119, 132, 134; Article 18, 99; Article 21, 99, 152; Article 44, 131; Article 47, 128; Article 58, 103; Article 63, 136; Article 67, 107; Article 81, 107, 136; Bonn, 98; federal, 87, 97; French (1946) (1958), 95; German Empire, 87; Prussion, 37; U.S.A., 87; Weimar, 9, 87, 97–98, 100

Constitutional Plaint (Bundesverfassungsgerichtsgesetz), 150

Constitutionality, 103, 150

Control, federal, 90–91; international, 22

Controversy, 133

Cooperation, 139

Coordination, 122

Coronation, 2

Corridor, 4

Corruption, 132

Council of Elders (Altestenrat), 127, 129, 132, 134; of Europe, 62; Legislative, of the District (Kreistag), 159; Parliamentary, 44, 48, 88; of State, 147; of States (Laenderrat), 32

Councillor, 159

County (Kreis), 57, 158

Court(s), 96, 128, 143; administra-

(Continued)
tive (Fed.), 145–149; civilian, 133; commercial chamber, 146; composition of, 146; Federal Constitutional 68–69, 98–100, 103–104, 127, 145–146, 148–149; Federal Finance, 148–149; Land Supreme (Bavaria), 146; Laender, 145–146; Patent (Fed.), 148; regional, 147; Social Security (Fed.), 148; Superior Regional, 146–147; Supreme Court for Labor Affairs (Fed.), 148; Supreme Federal, 147, 149: jurisdiction of, 147, Supreme Election committee, 147

Crisis, 55–56

Critisism, 49

Crown, 2; Imperial, 4

Culture, 1

Cuno, Wilhelm, 10

Currency, 90; reform, 45

Curzon Line, 19

Customs, 90

Czechoslovakia, 16, 83

Czechs, 2

Dachau, 15, 25

Danes, 2

de Gaulle, Charles, 52, 56–58, 85

Debate, 139; current events hour, 140

Decay, 2

Decree, presidential, 13

Defense, 58, 90, 93; Commissioner, 132, 134; Minister, 133, 157; National Council, 113

Dehler, Thomas, 65–67

Demilitarization, 23

Democracy, 8, 38, 88, 104, 132, 138; parliamentary, 102, 156; Western, 50

Denazification, 2, 25, 27, 114; American, British, French, Soviet, 26

Depression, 155

Deputy, 125, 130, 138, 140

Deutsche Angestellten-Gewerkschaft (DAG), 80

Deutsche Mark, 49

Deutscher Beamtenbund (DBB), 80

Dictatorship, 6, 7, 38, 41, 83

Diet, Prussian, 37

Disarmament, 22
Discipline, 60; action, 128
Discrimination, 96
Disraeli, Benjamin, 1
Dissension, 72
Dissolution, 136–137; political parties, 152
District, 159
Doenitz. Karl, 20
Doering, Wolfgang, 66
Duesseldorf, 66, 72; Principles of, 45
Dufhues, Hermann, 56
Dulles, Allen, 16–17
Dulles, John Foster, 54

East Berlin, 29, 162
East Germany, 28, 30, 45, 59, 83, 85–86, 100, 162
East Prussia, 4, 20, 79
Economic miracle, 94
Education, 47, 90, 93, 97; Communist, 85; legal, 115
Ehlers, Hermann, 46, 127
Eisenhower, Dwight, 22, 54
Elbe River, 60
Election, Americanization, 126; campaign, 61, 71; candidate, 125; d'Hondt system, 123; federal president, 161; Land, 58, 68; list system, 122; local, 61; national, 61; opposition, 76; plurality system, 122; proportional representation, 122–125; rallies, 71; regional, 61; run-off, 13; single member district, 125; split system, 125; validity, 151
Elections, 3, 42, 44, 54. 56, 70, 106, 132, 139; of 1949, 77; of 1953, 77; of 1957, 77; of 1961, 67, 75–77; of 1965, 63, 67, 72, 74–77, 110
Elector (Kurfürst), 3
Electorate, 78
Elizabeth of Russia, 5
Emergency, legislative (Gesetzgebungsnotstand), 107, 120, 136–137; power, 10, 136; proclamation, 137
Emperor, 3, 8, 9, 39–40; of Austria, 4
Empire, 3, 7, 119, 154; Second, 8
Engels, Friedrich, 6, 38

Enterprise, free, 49, 62; publicly owned, 45
Erhard, Ludwig, 45–49, 51–53, 55–58, 64, 69, 70–73, 76–77, 105, 111, 113, 131, 140–141; power, 110; international reputation, 110
Erler, Fritz, 71, 76, 141; chairman, parliamentary group, 63; education, 63
Ermeland, 4
Equality of men and women, 96
Equalization, 92
Eschenburg, Theodor, 111
Establishment, military, 55
Ethics, Christian, 44, 62
Etzel, Franz, 53
Europe, 39, 49, 56–57; Eastern, 82–83; United, 84
European Advisory Commission, 19
Europeans, 84
EURATOM, 84
Executive, 96, 132, 136; power, 102
Ex-Nazi, 66
Expellees, 79
Experimentation, Socialist, 74
Export, 49
Extradition, 90

Farmers' Federation, 81
Fascist, 6
Faulhaber, Cardinal, 48
Feder, Gottfried, 12
Federal Administration, 112
Federal Constitutional Court, 152, 153, 157, 161; composition, 149–150; decisions, 151; functions, 151; judges, 149–150; sections (Senate), 149–150
    See also Courts
Federal Council, see Bundesrat
Federal Diet, see Bundestag
Federal Republic, 44, 84, 88, 97, 99–102, 105, 107–108, 114, 116, 123, 126, 133, 138, 154; citizens, 83; Laender relationship, 89; territorial subdivisions, 89; unity, 104
Federalism, 15, 88, 119, 155, 157
Federation, 7; German, 87; industry, 109; North German, 38; peasant, 109; relationship, 150
Fleiner, Fritz, 117
Folklore, 4

Forces, police, 91
Forfeiture, basic rights, 99
Fraktion, see Parliamentary Group
France, 3, 19, 33, 52, 56–58, 82, 112, 147, 155; Council of State, 148
Francis I of Habsburg, 4
Francis II of Habsburg, 4
Franconia, 2
Frankfurt, 6, 33, 44, 89
Frederick I, King of Prussia, 5
Frederick II, Hohenstaufen, 3
Frederick II, "The Great," King of Prussia, 5
Frederick William, the "Great Elector," 5
Frederick William I, 5
Free German Committee, 27
Freedom, 86; academic, 98; of expression, 83; of press, 7, 83; of speech, 7
French, 158, 160; Fourth Republic, 105; National Assembly, 34, 127; Third Republic, 105
Frick, Wilhelm, 14

Gasperi, Alcide de, 84
General Staff, 8
German army, 133; Democratic Republic, 83, 97; economic unit, 33; educational system, 94, 114; electoral system, 125; Empire, 112; Farmers' Federation, 79; Federal Republic, 34, 45, 82, 118, 155, 156, 161; federalism, 87, 94; federation of industry, 79; history, 82; Labor Federation (DGB), 79–80; Labor Union Movement (CGB), 80; language, 82; military attaché, 55; Municipal Code of 1935, 155; nation, 2; national interest, 61; parliamentary system, 141; penal code, 128; people, 2, 84; policy, 75; poltics, 81; society, 31; Trade Union Federation, 78; unity, 4, 35
Germany, 1, 3, 4, 6; dismemberment, 22; division, 20, 30, 36; freedom, 35; reconstruction, 80; reunification, 33, 36; self-determination, 35
Gerstenmaier, Eugen, 46, 77, 127
Gestapo, 15–17
Globke, Hans, 109, 111

Goering, Hermann, 14, 88
Gold, 49
Goslar, 44
Gotha, 38
Government, 39, 55, 78, 130, 134, 136; Allied Military, 155; coalition, 122; control, 60, 139–140; crisis, 67; federal, 90–91, 120, 122, 150; French, 19; function of, 144; guidelines, 120; Laender, 93; Land, 122, 150, 154; local, 158, 160, 162; military, 19, 21, 32, 48, 59, 115; parliamentary, 45; policy, 65; West Berlin, 160; West German, 33; Western, 54
Great Britain, 19, 33, 49, 56, 57, 106; Corrupt Practices Act, 126; military governor, 48
Grievance, army, 133
Grosser, Alfred, 86
Grotewohl, Otto, 29–30
Group of the Center, 37
Guelphs, 38
Guttenberg, Karl Theodor Frieherr zu, 73

Habeas corpus procedure, 96
Hallstein, Walter, 51
Hamburg, 63, 70, 90, 118, 156
Hassel, Kai Uwe von, 133, 157
Health, municipal, 160
Heidenheimer, A., 121, 143
Hellwege, Heinrich, 157
Hertling, Count Karl von, 39
Hesse, Hermann, 70, 87–88, 90, 118, 121, 155, 156
Hessia, N., Minister of Interior, 59
Heuss, Theodor, 50, 52, 103–104; Chairman FDP, 65
Heye, Hellmuth, 133
Hindenburg, Paul von, 8, 9, 13–14, 48, 102
Hitler, Adolf, 1, 7, 12, 14–17, 39, 48; movement, 10; regime, 40, 114
Hochmeister, 4
Hohenstaufen, 3
Holland, 3
Holy Roman Empire of the German Nation, 2, 4, 7
House of Commons (British), 126
Hundhammer, Alois, 47
Hungary, 83

Identity, 83, 85; historical, 90
Immunities (Art. 46), 127; parliamentary, 128
Impeachment, 151
Imprisonment, 48
Independence, 60
Industry, 78; iron, 79; steel, 79
Inflation, 11, 13
Influence, Catholic, 77
Inquiry, 139–140
Instruction, religious, 97
Integration, 47, 60; European, 64, 67, 75
Intellectuals, 6
Interest groups, 78
Interference, 104; Anglo-Saxon, 56
Interpellation, 139
Invasion, 20
Investigations, 131
Iron Chancellor, 7
Isolation, 54
Israel, 16, 58
Italy, 3, 21

Jaeger, Richard, 73
Japan, 49
Jews, 12
Judge, 96, 143, 146–147, 149; lay, 144, 146; removal, 151
Judiciary, 94, 143; state, 144
Junkers, 5
Jurisdiction, original, 146; appeal, 146
Jurisprudence, 144
Jury, 146
Justice, social, 62

Kaisen, Wilhelm, 157
Kant, Immanuel, 95
Kassel, 148
Karlsruhe, 64, 147, 149
Kennedy, John F., 54
Kiesinger, Kurt Georg, 157
King-dictator, 5
Koenigsberg (Kaliningrad), 20
Kopf, Heinrich, 157
Kreisau Circle, 44
Krone, Heinrich, 52, 58, 113
Kuehlmann-Stumm, Knut von, 77

Labor Court, 148
    See also Courts
Labor Union, 96, 109, 136; movement, 80
Land, Laender, 7, 32, 44, 61, 64, 75, 88, 90–94, 97, 113, 118, 144, 147–148, 150–151, 159–162; administration, 116; agencies, 122; autonomy, 154; bureaucracy, 112, 121; cabinets, 121, 156; Constitutional Court, 150; constitutions, 107; Council, 33; courts, 112; elections, 93, 121, 157; finance courts, 149; government, 93, 120–122, 155, 156, 158; institutions, 115; legislature, 102, 156; mayor, 156; Minister of Justice, 147; Minister-President, 156; parliaments, 88; party list, 123; princes, 119; seats, 123; self-government, 157; Senate, 156; single member district, 123; subdivisions, 112
    See also Parties
Language, 1, 2
Landkreis, 160
Landsmannschaften (Regional Groupings), 79; meetings, 79
Lasalle, Ferdinand, 38
Law, 5, 135, 138, 145; anti-Socialist, 38; civil, 90; codes, 143; criminal, 90; electoral, 69; federal, 150; international 150; labor, 90; Land, 150; public, 151; procedure, 143; rules, 144; school, 144; telecommunication, 151; unification, 147
"Law and Order," 5
"Law for the Liberation from National-Socialism and Militarism," 25
Lawlessness, 95
Lawyers, 143
Lay Judges 144, 146
Leader, 45
Legislation, 93, 96, 131, 134, 137; federal, 91
Legislative Emergency (Gesetzgebungsnotstand), 136
Legislature, 118, 130; bicamerel, 118; convocation, 132; dissolution, 132, 136; Landtag, 156
Lenz, Otto, 109
Leuschner, Wilhelm, 59

Liability, state, 148
Libel, 128
Liberalism, 7; German, 6, 65
Liebknecht, Karl, 40
Liebknecht, Wilhelm, 38
Lingua Teutonica, 2
Lobby, 109, 122, 130, 138
London, 160; Conference, 33
Lorraine, 38
"Lost Provinces," 82
Lower Saxony, 68, 70, 90, 118, 156
Loyalty, 98
Ludendorff, Erich, 8–9
Luebke, Heinrich, 53, 104
Luxemburg, Rosa, 40
Luxembourg, 33

Madrid, 55
Magdeburg, 3
Maidanek, 15
Maier, Rheinhold, 66
Majority, 39–40, 60, 64, 105, 134,
    137, 139–140, 149; absolute, 107;
    Bundesrat, 119; Catholic, 47;
    Christian Democratic, 89; negative,
    107; party, 111; Social Democratic,
    89
Management, 148; industrial, 80
Margravate of Brandenburg, 4
Marshall Plan, 84
Marx, Karl, 6, 38
Marx, Wilhelm, 13
Masovia, Conrad of, 4
Martyrdom, 44
Mayor, 47, 158; of Bremen, 32; of
    Hamburg, 32
McCulloch vs. Maryland, 151
Mein Kampf, 12
Mende, Erich, 66–67, 72, 77, 78, 110
Merkatz, Hans Joachim von, 68
Metternich, 6
Michaelis, Georg, 39
Middelhauve, Friedrich, 65
Middle Ages, 84
Migration, 90
Military government, 24
    See also Government
Minister, 103, 109, 139; Agriculture,
    53, 114; Air, 88; CSU, 47; Cul-
    ture, 37; Defense, 47, 54, 57–58;
    Economics, 49, 111; Education,
    94; Family Affairs and Youth, 114;

federal, 108; Finance, 53; Foreign,
    51, 55–56, 72, 84, 110–111; Jus-
    tice, 65, 114, 145; State, 111; with-
    out portfolio, 52
Ministries, appointments, 81; federal
    116; Affairs of the Federal Coun-
    cil of the Laender 113; Economic
    Cooperation, 113; Family and
    Youth, 113; Finance, 113; Health,
    113; Nationalized Property, 113;
    Science, 113; Special Tasks, 113;
    State, 113
Ministry (Federal), All German
    Questions, 112; Defense, 112,
    131–132; Economics, 112; Finance,
    112; Food, Agriculture and Fores-
    try, 112, 116; Foreign Affairs, 112,
    131; Housing, 112; Interior, 112;
    Justice, 112; Labor and Social Af-
    fairs, 112; Post and Transport,
    112; Refugees, Escapees and Dis-
    abled Veterans, 112
Misconduct, 132
Mismanagement, 132
Moabit Prison, 44
Monnet, Jean, 84
Morgenthau, Hans, 22
Morgenthau Plan, 23
Moscow, 19, 82
Mueller, Josef, 47
Multiparty system, 105, 122, 137
Munich, 11, 57, 148, 149
Municipality, 154, 160
Münster, 3

Nation, 1
National Assembly, 6
Nationalism, 7, 12, 67, 77, 84
Nationalists, 14–16, 37, 40
Nationality, 90
Nationalization, 62; of industry, 74
NATO, 75, 133
Nazi, 6, 14, 57, 143, 152; atrocities,
    145; criminals, 144; infiltration, 65;
    movement, 68; party, 13, 14, 15,
    107; period, 40, 63, 94; regime,
    25, 95, 97, 114, 147–148, 154,
    157; voters, 68
Nazis, 15, 29, 37, 44, 58, 158
Nazism, 12, 19, 22, 86, 88
Neisse River, 20
Netherlands, 33, 40

Neutrality, 143
Newspaper, 144
Nonattendance, penalty, 128
Nonconfidence, vote, 132
North-Rhine Westphalia, 46, 70, 90, 118, 127, 156, 159
Norway, 62

Objection to military service, 96
Obligations of Land, 92
Occupation, 23, 60, 160; agreement, 21; allied, 20, 31, 88; authorities, 22, 8, 88; directive, 3; military, 27, 31; policy, 7–8; Russian, 27–28; Statute, 33–34, 89, 161; Western, 27, 31; Zone, 8
Oder River, 20–21
Offices, local, 91; regional, 91
Ollenhauer, Erich, 60–63, 141
Opinion polls, 92; public, 145
Opposition, 61, 89, 139, 157; intra-party, 58, 72; loyal, 75; nationalist, 72, 77; party, 71, 139
Order, democratic, 99; executive, 119
Order of Teutonic Knights, 4
Organization, power, 138; refugee, 79, 81; veterans', 79
    See also Bundesrat; Bundestag
Osnabrück, 3

Palermo, 3
Pan-Europe Movement, 84
Papen, Franz von, 14
Paris, 9, 16, 160
Parliament, 7–9, 15, 37, 39, 44, 53, 72, 79, 102–103, 106, 112, 130, 138, 145; Building (Bundeshaus), 126; committees, 129; control, 139; dissolution, 107; federal, 58; French, 126; German, 13; Prussian, 38; seat, 78, 122
    See also Bundestag
Parliamentary Council, 89, 97, 122, 144
Parliamentary Group (Fraktion), 55, 58, 67, 129, 131, 136; Chairman, 51; influence, 140; leader (Fraktionsvorsitzender), 140
    See also Council
Partition, Germany, 59
Party, bureaucracy, 63–64; candidacy, 125–126; chairman, 55–56, 62, 65,

(Continued)
    73, 108; committee (SPD), 60; conduct, 79; conference (SPD), 59; congress (SPD), 62, 63, 64; council, 76; deputy, 79, 81; deputy chairman, 58, 63; discipline, 78, 80; executive chairman, 56; executives, 138; extremist, 138; followers, 78; general secretary (CDU), 57; group, 125; interest, 121; leader, 51, 81, 106, 125, 130; leadership, 40, 48, 51, 55, 59–60, 62, 64, 74, 76, 78, 139; local, 125; majority leader, 73; membership 116; nominations, 125; passports, 90; political, 27–28, 42, 106; politics, 74, 121; president (CSU), 58; press, 41; program, 62; public image, 130; rebellion, 110; standard bearer, 62; struggle, 76; system, 125; tradition, 77
Paulus, Field Marshal Friedrich von, 27
People's Court, 95
Persecution, 39, 62
Peter III of Russia, 5
Petersberg Protocol, 34
Pieck, Wilhelm, 27
Plauen, Henry von, 4
Plurality, 64, 106, 125
Poincaré, Raymond, 10
Poland, 5, 19, 21, 38, 83; Duke of, 4
Poles, 2, 4, 38
Police, criminal, 90
Policy, 54, 60, 106, 138; Allied Military Government, 41; defense, 76; departmental, 108; domestic, 71; European, 58; foreign, 47, 49, 51, 57, 71, 73, 76, 82; general, 108–109; post-Stalinist, 82; social, 45; Western, 73
Political parties, Action Group of Independent Germans (AUD), 69
    All German Federation—Federation of the Homeless and Disenfranchised (GD/BHE), 68
    Bavarian (BP), 45, 69
    Catholic, 44
    Center, 7, 13, 37–41, 44–45
    Christian Democrats, 41, 44, 76, 157

(*Continued*)
Christian Democratic Union (CDU), 29, 37, 41, 44, 46–48, 51–53, 55, 58, 60–61, 65–75, 77, 88, 108, 110, 121–122, 127, 131, 133, 137, 140
Christian Social Union (CSU), 41, 44, 46–47, 51, 53, 57–58, 60–61, 67–74, 110, 131, 133, 137, 140
Communist (KPD), 69, 99, 107
Free Democratic (FDP), 46, 54–55, 64–68, 70, 72, 74, 77–78, 103, 110, 113, 131, 137, 157
Free Social Union (FSU), 69
French Popular Republican Movement (MRP), 41
German (DP), 68
German Nationalist, 11
German Peace Union (DFU), 69
German People's, 64
German Reich (DRP), 68
Liberal Democratic, 29
National Democratic (NPD), 68
Nazi, *see* Nazi
Social Democratic (SPD), 7, 28, 29, 37–40, 46, 49, 52, 55, 58–71, 74–78, 80, 88–89, 104–105, 110, 116, 121–122, 131, 133, 137, 139, 140, 157
Socialist Unity (SED), 29, 161
Socialist Reich (SRP), 99
Pollock, James K., 32
Polls, 75
Pope, 3, 38
Population, 60, 88
Positivism, legal, 143
Potsdam Agreement, 33; Conference, 19
Powers, Allied, 19, 89, 161; Central, 90; federal, 151; fiscal, 155; foreign, 97; Western, 33, 125
Presidency, 52, 53, 77
President, 47, 50, 52, 105–107, 136; election, 104; power, 103, 127; term, 102
Press, 96
Pressure groups, 78–79, 81
Preuss, Hugo, 2
Prime Minister, 7, 102
Principality, 119
Privileged communications, 128

Probst, Christoph, 17
Production, 49
Prohibition, of Communist Party, 152; of Socialist Reich Party, 152
Proportional representation, 123
Protestants, 4, 38, 44, 77, 116, 127
Prussia, 4–7, 14, 38, 48, 87, 90, 156; abolition, 88; Duchy of, 4; minister president, 88; predominance, 119; prime minister, 119
Prussian administration, 87; bureaucracy, 87
Pruzzen, 4

Quadripartite Allied Control Commission, 29–30
Quebec Conference, 23

Radicalism, 11
Radio, 93
Railroad traffic, 90
Ramke, General, 79
Ravensbruck, 15
Rearmament, 61
Rebellion of July 20, 1944, 44, 68
Reconciliation, Franco-German, 50
Reconstruction, 49, 84
Redress (*Verfassungsbeschwerde*), 99
Refugees, 79
Regensburg, 94
Regime, Communist, 82–83; democratic, 83, 116; East German, 83; Nazi, 59–60
Registration, voters, 126
Rehabilitation, 72, 84
Rehmer, Ernst, 68
Reich, 2, 4, 102, 155; cabinet, 119; chancellor, 48; German, 38; government, 91; president, 136; second, 38; sovereignty, 119
Reichsrat, 119
Reichstag, 13–15, 39; building, 126
Relations, East-West, 33, 54, 76; Franco-German, 57
Relationship, executive-legislative, 138
Religion, 96, 116
Renan, Ernest, 1
Rentenmark, 11
Representation, proportional, 102
Repression, 83
Republic, 49; French Third and

(*Continued*)
Fourth, 10; German, 9, 48;
Weimar, 9–10
Resignation, 55–56
Resistance, 44
Retirement, 48
Reunification, 49–50, 60–61, 81, 85–86
Revolt, 17, 19
Revolution, 38; of 1848, 6, 87;
French, 6
Rhine, 21, 89
Rhineland, 48, 156
Rhineland-Palatinate, 70, 88, 90, 118, 121, 156
Rhineland-Westphalia, 66
Rhoendorf, 48, 89
Right, 45; government, 96; man, 6;
property, 96
"Right of codetermination," 148
Roman Empire, 2
Rome, 2
Roosevelt, Franklin D., 19, 23
Rothfels, Hans, 16
Ruhr, 5, 10, 70, 156
Rumania, 21, 83
Run-off election, 13
Russia, 9, 19, 30, 39
    See also Soviet Union
Russians, 41, 50, 61, 125, 160–161

Saar, 65, 118
Saarland, 31, 50, 69–70, 90, 155–156
St. Paul's Church, 6
Satellite, 30, 32–33
Saxon, 2
Saxony, 68; Duke of, 3
Schaeffer, Fritz, 47
Scheel, Walter, 66
Schleicher, Kurt von, 14
Schleswig-Holstein, 90, 118, 121, 156
Schmid, Carlo, 63–64, 104, 131
Schmidt, Helmut, 76
Scholl, Hans, 17
Scholl, Inge, 17
Scholl, Sophie, 17
Schools, Catholic, 98; elementary, 98;
nonconfessional, 97; nonreligious, 98; private, 97–98; public, 97–98;
religious, 98; secondary, 115
Schroeder, Gerhard, 46, 53, 56–58, 71–73, 77, 110–111

Schumacher, Kurt, 29, 46, 50, 59–61, 75, 89, 104
Schuman, Robert, 50, 84, 165; Plan, 33, 75, 84
Science, 98
Seats, major parties (*Bundestag*), 42
Secrecy, 138; mail and telecommunications, 99
Secret Police, 27
Sector (Berlin), Russian, 161; security personnel, 127; Western, 161
Service, public, 114
Shrivenham, 22–23
Silesia, 79
Social Democrats, 14
    See also Party; Social Democratic
Socialism, 39, 62
Socialist, 16, 149
Sokolovsky, Marshall, 26
Soviet Union, 19–21, 50, 61, 65, 76, 86; army, 27
Soviets, 41
Spaak, Paul-Henri, 84
Speaker, 127
Spiegel, der, 55, 57
Stalin, Josef, 15, 19, 21; era, 76
Stalingrad, 20, 27
State, 2, 84, 87, 97; rights, 93, 157;
secretaries, 109
State Council, Prussian, 47
Statistics, education, 129
Statute of Limitations, 144–145
Statutes, 154
Stauffenberg, Klaus Werner von, 17–18
Steel, 49
"Steel Helmet," 11
Stettin, 20
Strauss, Franz Josef, 47, 54–55, 57, 71–73, 76, 110, 133
Stresemann, Gustav, 64, 68
Strike Fund, 81
Structure, 2; coalition, 113; federal, 112–113; government, 122
Stuttgart, 32
Subsidies, 45, 161, 162
Succession, 51–52, 77; crisis, 67
Sudetenland, 79
Suffrage, 8
Supervision, 92, 132; Laender, 91;
parliamentary, 134

Support, local, 78
Suppression, political party, 151
Switzerland, 10, 109

Tannenberg, Battle of, 4
Taxes, 154; income, 92, 154
Teaching, freedom of, 98
Television, 93; interview, 73; network, 151
Thaelmann, Ernst, 13
"Theodisk," 1
Third French Republic, 105
Third Reich, 7, 95
Trade Union, 148; Catholic, 80; Christian Movement 46; president, 59
Trademark and copyright, 90
Transportation system, 160
Treason, 55, 147
Treaty, 134; of Bonn, 34; ratification, 119, 135
Treschkow, Henning von, 17–18
Trial, deputy, 128
Two-party system, 41, 66, 77, 105, 126
Tyranny, 39

Ulbricht, Walter, 27, 30, 83
Unconstitutionality, 99
Unification, German, 33, 36; European, 62
Union, federal, 88; German Officers, 27
Unions, 138
United Europe, 166
United States, 19, 22, 33, 49, 54, 56–58, 96, 131, 160; administrative system, 112; army, 57, 133; authorities, 87; Chiefs of Staff, 23; Congressmen, 78; constitution, 90; Corrupt Practices Act, 126; Defense Department, 22; economic aid, 32; embassy, 49; Federal Accounting Office, 148; government, 22, 112; jurisdiction, 87; policy, 25; political science, 81; president, 54, 102; presidential system, 102; Senate, 93; Senators, 78; separation of federal, state, local government, 154; State Department, 22, 23, 112; Supreme Court, 98; War Department, 23

Unity, 1, 5, 86; economic, 91; German, 7; legal, 91; Western, 50, 61
University, 115, 144; Bonn, 131; Cologne, 131; degree, 114; funds, 94; professors, 94; students, 94
Utilities, 160

Versailles Treaty, 10
Veto, 136; absolute, 135; suspensive, 135
Vice-Chancellor, 59, 67, 109–110
Vienna, 160
Vote, 53, 55, 59, 66, 134; confidence, 107, 140; nonconfidence, 106; first, 123; second 123; CDU/CSU, 145; FDP, 145; SDP, 145
    See also Parties
Voters, 45, 75, 125; middle class, 74; Protestant, 47
Votes (1949-1965), statistics, 42

Wages, 45
Wahllokomotive (election engine), 70
Wall, Berlin, 54, 82, 162
War, crimes, 144–145; Franco-Prussian, 6, 7, 82; Napoleonic, 4; Thirty Years', 3; World War I, 8, 39, 60, 82; World War II, 51, 63, 84, 88, 116, 155
Washington, 54, 160; Conference, 33
Wehner, Herbert, 63, 76
Weimar, 44, 66, 132, 138
Weimar regime, cause of failure, 141
Weimar Republic, 11, 14, 24, 28, 37, 40, 48, 59–60, 64, 80, 105, 108, 112, 114, 119, 122, 128, 143, 148, 154, 157; Constitution, 2, 91, 96, 129, 137; Dictatorship Article (48), 136; period, 16, 84, 127; president, 102
Welfare, public, 160
West Berlin, 118, 156; cabinet (Senate), 162; chief executive, 162; district government, 162; district mayor, 162; House of Representatives, 162; composition of, 162
West Germany, 28, 30, 59, 65
West Prussia, 4
Western Allies, 28
Westphalian Peace, 3–4

Westrick, Ludger, 11, 113
William II, Emperor of Germany, 7
Wirtschaftswunder (Economic Miracle), 48
Wuerttemberg, 65–66
Yalta Conference, 19

Zinn, Georg August, 157
Zone, Allied, 32; American, 25, 27, 32–33; British, 31–33; French, 31–33, 155; Occupation, 21–22, 24; Soviet, 27, 29, 31–33, 36; Western, 28, 33, 41, 155